Remember

Divine Healings, Unassisted Childbirths,
Victory over Demons, a Live Liver Donation, and More—
Discover God's Powerful Love through
These Inspiring Lessons and Miracles.

ROXANNE MUNSEN

WESTBOW
P R E S S
A DIVISION OF THOMAS NELSON

WestBow Press books may be ordered through booksellers or by contacting:

WestBow Press
A Division of Thomas Nelson
1663 Liberty Drive
Bloomington, IN 47403
www.westbowpress.com
1 (866) 928-1240

Because of the dynamic nature of the Internet, any web addresses or
links contained in this book may have changed since publication and
may no longer be valid. The views expressed in this work are solely those
of the author and do not necessarily reflect the views of the publisher,
and the publisher hereby disclaims any responsibility for them.

Certain stock imagery © Thinkstock.
Any people depicted in stock imagery provided by Thinkstock are models,
and such images are being used for illustrative purposes only.

Unless otherwise noted, all scriptures are taken from the King James Bible.

ISBN: 978-1-4908-1261-8 (e)
ISBN: 978-1-4908-1260-1 (sc)
ISBN: 978-1-4908-1259-5 (hc)

Library of Congress Control Number: 2013918584

Printed in the United States of America.

WestBow Press rev. date: 10/18/2013

For Nyomi, Malachi, Courage, Prudence, Josiah, Titus, and all the following generations to come. We love you and hope you can learn from our lives: to not repeat our mistakes and abound in faith, hope, and love.

"Love should be the silver thread that runs through all your conduct. Kindness, gentleness, long-suffering, forbearance, patience, sympathy, a willingness to enter into childish troubles, a readiness to take part in childish joys —these are the chords by which a child may be led most easily—these are the clues you must follow if you would find the way to his heart."
- J.C. Ryle, British Prime Minister and author, from _The Upper Room_, 1888

TABLE OF CONTENTS

Foreword ix

Acknowledgements...xi

Introduction xiii

Chapter 1   Nyomi Shanook Munsen 1

Chapter 2   Malachi Edward Munsen...9

Chapter 3   Two Miracles, One for Each Day........................ 15

Chapter 4   The Lies of the Fish Story 23

Chapter 5   Courage James Munsen.. 31

Chapter 6   To Box or Not to Box? That is the Question 45

Chapter 7   Accelerated Learning, Part I:
                 The prelude to life-long lessons............................ 57

Chapter 8   Prudence Evelyn Munsen 63

Chapter 9   The Commandments 73

Chapter 10   Accelerated Learning, Part II:
                 Lessons Learned... 85

Chapter 11   Being about God's Business................................ 95

Chapter 12   Victory over Darkness.. 105

Chapter 13   Concerning Tithe and Provisions 113

Chapter 14   Will a Cloth hold us back?.................................123

Chapter 15   A Transplant, If You Please 133

Chapter 16   Josiah Ray Munsen 141

Chapter 17   Deliverance... 151

Chapter 18   The Story of Brayden 157

Chapter 19   Wanted: A Willing Vessel for my Service 163

Chapter 20   Titus Robert Munsen.. 169

Chapter 21   A Note on Child Training................................... 181

Chapter 22   Exorcisms and our Free Will 191

Chapter 23   Not the Beginning or the End,
                       Just the Middle 201

Appendix I   Interview with my dearly beloved
                       Lucas Munsen..207

Appendix II   Luke's On-the-Mountain Prayer Notes 211

Appendix III   Character Qualities 215

Appendix IV   A Few Fun Home Remedies and
                       Other Recipes 217

Contact Information..221

FOREWORD

When Roxanne approached me to review *Remember*, I didn't think too much about it until she presented it to me. As I read this autobiography of her beautiful family, I kept asking myself over and over again, "Why me? Why did she ask me?"

I've only known the Munsen family for about three years. At first, I had my curiosity of this family, but as I grew to know them, my curiosity became respect. I witnessed the love between Roxanne and Luke, their last two pregnancies, and their four children excel each time they came to the library.

I found *Remember* to be comforting. The way it built and flowed through each chapter gave me a sense of calming. I didn't want to put it down. It's a spiritual book with stories of miracles, their own challenges, and their strong belief and faith in God. My four children have already chosen their paths, but I've been blessed with five grandchildren and a great grandbaby. *Remember* gives me the courage to pass some of this comfort and wisdom on to another generation.

With my own belief in God, I would pray to Him every night, asking Him to help me find happiness in my life, He finally did, Roxanne's book, *Remember*. *Remember* is telling me that God wants me to enjoy my life by spending time with Him, reading His word, praying and listening for His direction. I now know why Roxanne asked me to read her book: it was God's way of answering my prayers. There are reasons why certain people cross our paths.

I would highly recommend *Remember* to anyone that feels there is no hope in their lives or just to help them find their own paths. I hope that everyone who reads this book will enjoy the journey as I did.

Being Honest,

Sue Azevedo, Mullan, Idaho

ACKNOWLEDGEMENTS

My heart swells with praise, humility, thanksgiving, and reverent awe all at once for our Sweet Lord. Without Him we wouldn't have anything worth writing about. I am also grateful to have God's loving Holy Word to guide us and try the spirits as we walk with Him.

We wish to deeply thank everyone involved in editing this book to help it reach its completion. A very special thank you is due to Mrs. Evelyn Bear. God has gifted her with amazing editing talents, and I am very blessed to be the recipient of such ability.

I also desire to send my warmest regards and appreciation to our church families and friends, and those who have been a great source of encouragement as we strive to be in God's Will.

Thank you and we love you dearly.

"Error is old, but older still is the Truth that overcomes it."
~Unknown

Hi! To introduce ourselves, my husband is Lucas James Munsen, more commonly known as Luke. He is a healthy man with red hair and green eyes. He stands about five feet, eleven inches tall and weighs a fit two hundred pounds. His birth date is June 23, 1980. My name is Roxanne Lee Munsen, also known as Roxy. My birth date is February 28, 1981. I have been told I have red hair and I have been told I have blonde hair, but my driver's license says I have brown hair. I look forward to having a whole head of silver, preferably white. For the Bible says in Job 12:12, "With the ancient is wisdom; and in length of days understanding." I have so little now, to think I may have some someday is exciting! I am five feet seven inches tall and weigh some here and some more there according to my pregnancies and such. I met my beloved at eighteen years of age in August 1999, and we married July 22, 2000 (I was nineteen).

March 22, year 2003, our sweet and precious daughter was born. Her name is Nyomi Shanook Munsen. The name "Shanook" is special to probably only me as I had a dream concerning her. I would have named her that, but it was not a favorite among others.

It is a wonderful gift to me that Luke allowed her middle name to be *Shanook*. Our maiden Nyomi is a complete delight. She is my kitchen and sewing buddy. Among her accomplishments at age seven are having sewn a quilt, potholders, and several dresses. At age nine she sews her own wardrobe, can make several dishes for dinner, is our cracker maker, has designed her own healthy frosting, and began a glycerin soap making business that she owns and operates herself, including the basic business sheets. I look forward to her teenage-years where we will be great friends sharing all our endeavors together. However, the most exciting aspect about Nyomi is her heart. She has chosen to seek after filling it with God's holy word and His love, to live her life after Jesus Christ's example, and accept His sacrifice for her. It really manifests itself in the way she conducts herself toward her siblings and family. We love to see God working in her.

Our second child (born eighteen months later) is Malachi Edward Munsen (birth date September 24, 2004). "Edward" is after both his Grandpa David's middle name, and Grandpa David's dad's first name, Edward. We are excited about the gentleman he is becoming. He is quick to open the car door for his sisters and me. It's so wonderful to see he has learned the value of working hard so that play does not *always* come first in his heart. What a blessing for God to impress that upon him. At age eight, he proclaims he is training for missionary work whether that's in his home, neighborhood, country, abroad, or all the above. Just in case, he chooses to sleep on the hardwood floor, instead of a mattress, so he's ready when he's older. Malachi is currently asking for God to use him and reveal where He wants him to do his missionary work. With all the imperfection in our family members and especially our own parenting, it is a joyous blessing to watch God bless the fruits of our efforts. Really, if we seek first the kingdom of God, *with our children,* and follow Deuteronomy chapter six in that they remain in our shadow and under all authority, God will make our parenting "scribbles" into a work of art. Praises and glory to our Gracious Father!

July 6, 2006, brought along our third child and second boy. We named him Courage James Munsen. James is his daddy's middle name and it is also Luke's grandpa's middle name, Walter James Eastman. Courage is learning the benefits of overcoming laziness and focusing to become a hard-working diligent man. His choice to resiliently change his attitude to joy is quite inspirational. He is tender-hearted, a natural orator and loves to make others laugh. We are enjoying his continual love as well as seeing his new interest in choosing God's ways.

Number four is our second daughter. May 3, 2008 brought the gift of Prudence Evelyn Munsen. "Evelyn" is after her great-grandmother Evelyn Munsen. That Evelyn was wife to Edward and mother to David, Luke's dad. Prudence has red hair and looks like her daddy. She is quick with a smile and has been a ray of sunshine in our lives. Her spunky personality and wit unintentionally provides much mirth in the family. She furthermore exhibits a very frank and matter-of-fact way of speech and life. If there is any help needed, she is the first to bounce over and offer!

March 20, 2010, we celebrated the birth of our fifth child and third boy. His name is Josiah Ray Munsen. "Ray" is in honor of his grandpa's—my dad's—middle name. He was born with lots of brown hair and a dark complexion. He loves to smile and laugh, and make a lot of other noise, too. He is our busiest member, always finding a way to keep his hands occupied. He is still learning, however, that busy hands need to be industrious and not mischievous!

The year of 2012 saw us blessed with another soul to nurture. God granted us a boy on February 2. Titus Robert Munsen is our fourth boy, fifth homebirth, and sixth child. We are so grateful that God will allow such births to happen. To take us through healthy prenatal care and pregnancies and then smoothly and safely bring forth this newly created life is awe-inspiring in the least! Oh, how thankful we are for this! Titus' middle name, Robert, carries forth Grandpa Bob's first name, Robert. Robert Chitwood, or Bob, is Luke's stepdad. So far, Titus appears to have my black and white attitude. This means things are superbly great or they are bad. I will continue to work on myself so I can better help him on his way. At merely a year of age though, I could be wrong about him.

My beloved and I have grown considerably under the patience and love of our Heavenly Father. It is our duty and pleasure, not the state's, to nurture, train, and teach our children of God's ways. Deuteronomy 32:46 says "set your hearts unto all the words which I testify among you this day, which ye shall command your children to observe to do, all the words of this law." In doing this we feel they also need to *remember* what God has done for us. God does not want us to *live* in the past, but to remember what He has done for us. The Passover is a great example of that—when He afterward commanded generations to be told of the event forever.

We feel very humbled to be a part of God's plan. Several times we have gathered as a family to recount the ways God has been active in our lives. It wasn't until 2008 though, that we felt the urgent need to record the stories so we could keep our testimony alive for our children, and the multi-generations to come. So, without having any prior writing experience, we have compiled our growth chronologically. After four and a-half years, we suddenly feel a green light to publish.

We hope these lessons and stories will be passed down as part of an inheritance and testimony of our *Living* God. We believe it is important to share our experiences of guidance, blessings, miracles, lessons, and chastisements to aid the next leap of faith. We want you, and the additions to the family through marriage, to understand that the Holy Spirit, through the *Bible,* will guide you through anything in life. God's Word contains inspired answers, encouragements, and warnings to teach and give you all you need to know. You do not need *man, book,* or *CD* next to the Bible to help interpret it, and that includes this book we are writing. All you need is the Holy Ghost whom Jesus sent after he ascended. Don't follow man's interpretation alone. Prove everything by the Bible. This means you must read it continually. Read this book for its miracles and faith. We want you to see the *real* intimate workings of the God of Abraham, Isaac, and Jacob in our lives and to know your Father in Heaven craves your relationship, too. You, too, need to feel comfortable allowing God to control, guide, and bless your lives. Yes, to live eternally in heaven with God also, but moreover, we wish you to live with the kingdom in you, in love, here on earth first. Read and have faith.

What I would really enjoy doing is spending the next moments writing to tell you of how wonderfully my husband steadfastly disciples his family with one goal: to bring us closer to Christ the best he can. However, this book is not about my husband, it is about something much *greater.* Although this book is written from my point of view, it is assembled by both my husband *and* myself—the two of us as one flesh under God. It will share miracles, testimonies, blessings, and lessons of God's intimate involvement as he renovates us to be holy habitations.

We will begin with the birth story of our first child.

CHAPTER 1

Nyomi Shanook Munsen

~ Born March 2003 ~

Two years after our marriage in July 2000, we lived in Spokane, Washington, in a boarding home for the elderly. We were paid room and board in return for caring for a few clients twice a week. Our total room size was fifteen feet by fifteen feet. It was here we were blessed with the pregnancy of our first child. We were so excited! We had set up a microwave and electric griddle as our kitchen in one of the bay windows (although we could use the home's kitchen too). We had two rocking chairs, our queen-size bed, a dorm-size fridge, a crib, and a dresser for the baby. The room also had a walk-in closet.

We idly talked of having our baby at home with a midwife where it wouldn't be exposed to all the variety of germs, infections, and interruptions in the hospital. However, before we ever told anyone else of these dreams, we heard from a few different family members who said, "I hope you aren't going to have the baby at home," and then why. So, we did what everyone else does and began prenatal appointments. After all, we'd never had a baby before.

As soon as we were ten weeks pregnant, we were on our way for yet another checkup. At this particular checkup, the doctor didn't hear anything. She immediately referred us to take an ultrasound "just to make sure nothing was wrong" as she wasn't able to make out anything. She proceeded to calmly explain how "sometimes this happens, and the baby is probably dead and hadn't aborted yet. No, don't blame yourself as nobody knows why these miscarriages happen. There are two things to do at this point: wait and let your body naturally expel the dead fetus or have a "D and C"—a procedure that surgically scrapes the uterus clean—but let's not panic yet and just get the ultrasound."

Well, Luke and I prayed together outside the doctor's office and acknowledged that we didn't need to be afraid, as this baby was in God's control. We asked for peace, faith, healing in our baby if there was anything wrong, and that God would allow it to live, but God's will be done. We had the ultrasound and the first one showed an unmoving blob. The nurse moved us to another machine because the first "was fuzzy." This machine didn't seem to work either at first, as she still couldn't make out what she was looking for. She eventually took her "pictures" anyhow and *finally* claimed that our baby was indeed healthy, well, and alive! No problems with it at all! We left rejoicing and never went to that doctor again. In fact, it wasn't until we were six months pregnant that we learned of some midwives affiliated with a hospital in Spokane. We had tried an ob-gyn, and the midwife sounded much better. So we began appointments with them. There were two midwives who shared appointments and the day you went into labor decided your attendant.

Some of the fun in pregnancies is trying to pick the perfect name. At one point I had asked God if He would allow me to envision my baby and to help us pick out a name. One night God granted me a vivid dream of my unborn child as a five, or six, year-old daughter. It was a dream that I hope to never forget, and I wish I could play it as a movie for my husband and others to see exactly for themselves just what I saw. Although the part I can remember is short, it's enough. I dreamed: I was a mother and gleefully playing tag with my daughter. We were at a family reunion. I teased at her departing form, racing away with shrieks of laughter. I remember it as such a beautiful and penetrating sound. She turned back to watch me with merriment in her eyes and I was amazed at how much she looked just like me. She had taken after me with the same freckles I have, the same features, and the same voice and laughter. She had the same gaiety and loved the same type of feminine flounce on her dress as she does today. Her hair was also full of body and curly waves, as it is today. However, the color was dark auburn rather than dark brown. She turned again and raced away, turning a sharp corner. "What an absolute joy," I thought. I was searching for her when I realized I could no longer hear her giggles. A panic began to well up at the thought of something happening to my precious daughter. I immediately began calling for her, "Shanook! Shanook?" It was a calm, drawn-out call, but my heart felt frozen with fear. "Shaaanooook!" All of a sudden she shrieked with glee at the fact that she had hidden so well and darted out from behind someone as we moved our game of chase to a more open area.

That small excerpt is all I can remember, but that same small memory is a vivid blessing from God. I shared it with Luke and asked if we could name her Shanook, but he didn't like the name at all. I remained persistent when the subject came around and didn't care what others thought. They hadn't seen "my little girl." I bargained that if it was a girl and she was born with red hair, could we name her Shanook? Luke decided upon the name Nyomi if we were blessed with a girl (and I equally enjoyed it) and we made

"Shanook" Nyomi's middle name. At the end of the pregnancy, Luke thought I was having a boy, but I was guessing it was a girl.

March 21, 2003 was my due date. Luke and I had walked regularly to prepare for the delivery process. The due date came and we proceeded to bed wondering how long we would have to wait. At one o'clock the next morning I awoke. The contractions began immediately. We were so excited that we couldn't sleep—not a good idea when in labor. We *should* have relaxed more to store up energy for the duration of the twenty-one hour labor and delivery. We made sure all our bags and paraphernalia were ready and took out our coloring books. We colored and timed the contractions. Nothing was terribly consistent, but the water kept draining in frequent intervals. We managed to nap a little more, and at seven o'clock in the morning we called the midwife. We didn't want to go in too early but decided to call for advice. She asked if any water had broken and at my confirmation of "a little," she was adamant that we come in. As my contractions were quite painful, I thought I was in at least stage two. I nearly took offense when we arrived at the hospital, and the midwife laughed and said I was only in stage one because "I was still smiling". Stage two means there are "no more smiles." Looking back now, I know she was right.

At the beginning of the prenatal appointments with the midwives we were to draw up a "birth plan" of how we wanted the atmosphere to be, what procedures we wanted and didn't want, who we wanted there, and how we wanted birth to happen. We wanted dim lights and soft music for relaxing, no constant checkups with the monitor or anything else (monitoring blood pressure and my heartbeat wasn't an option), and we only wanted the attending nurse and the midwife—no other onlookers, well-wishers, or doctors. However, when we arrived with our radio and pillows as planned, we realized that following our birth plan was going to be a fight. The midwife turned "institutional" on us. She started explaining how we only had a certain time frame in which to birth the baby before drastic measures would have to be employed—including cesarean. She insisted upon a blood pressure test and I tested high. I explained to her that it was because I was in the hospital, and that alone would raise it—not to mention the excitement and stress of her unexpected time limit for delivering the baby and other must-do procedures. She wasn't convinced and insisted upon a blood sample to further test for the baby's stress. I refused, and all the arguing she tried didn't budge me an inch. It was unnecessary, and that was the end of it. I wished I could leave the hospital, but I didn't think I could and didn't know what to do if I did leave. I felt cornered and trapped, when I only wanted privacy and silence. I was also quickly forgetting to be a Christian.

I evidently wasn't progressing enough and we consented to the water being broken to speed up the process (the bag had only torn at the top). I then learned what she meant by second stage of labor. Intensity immediately picked up. My experience was all back labor and as I described it to Luke: it felt like my back was in flames and someone was actually pulling the lumbar section away from my body. The hottest of towels didn't feel warm enough to ease the pain, but Luke was great. He stayed with me the entire time, talking when I needed to hear his loving voice and becoming my voice to stand our ground where staff was concerned.

The majority of this time I lay there as if sleeping, just the way we had practiced. (Luke and I never took childbirth classes, but studied and practiced ourselves with the Bradley Method. At the time, Lamaze Classes not only taught that the doctors know best, but also taught a new way of breathing and encouraged epidurals. The Bradley Method taught about childbirth itself and what happens in each stage—how to work *with* your body and not against it, and to rely on relaxing and breathing normally instead of in new patterns. It encouraged natural drugless childbirth. And of course, we did not want to use any drugs or epidurals.)

I began to cue the staff, and Luke, so they would know when a contraction was coming on. This meant *hands off!*—especially for the nurses. They seemed to think that since I was in the middle of a contraction, they could take my blood pressure from my leg instead of my arm. So now, during a hard contraction when I needed all energy to muster relaxing, I suddenly had someone lifting my leg to encircle my ankle with a blood pressure cuff—heedless of my laboring. These were regular nurses in the labor and delivery floor! You'd think they would know better! I had tried all day to communicate politely. Evidently, I thought I needed to trade-in Jesus for my carnal flesh to get through labor. Thus, with all nurses and midwifes present (and there were *several* coming in and out), I told Luke the plan. I would grunt at the first sign of every contraction. That was all the warning I could give and still have enough time to exhale and relax. Luke relayed the message across the bed to the midwife.

Before the pushing stage arrived, there was some color in the fluid and the midwife declared an emergency of "me conium." How we wished she trusted God, too, to avoid the hoop-la and drama of it all. Amongst all the coming and going of staff (I felt quite violated in the modesty department), a special cart was wheeled into the corner, and a team of nurses attentively waited to whisk the baby away to suck out its lungs, weigh it, warm it, check it, and whatever else they needed to do.

When the birth was actually at hand, I wanted to get off the bed but was told to stay. Not knowing what better to do, I stayed, but I *was not* lying down. The midwife consented and had me sit up. Still not comfortable, I regretfully remember resenting everyone in the room except Luke. I told myself it was because I wanted peace and quiet, but honestly, it was due to my selfish pride. At long last, I evidently reached some magic point and was told pushing would begin. Not feeling like it, I figured she knew best. The midwife started yelling, "PUSH!" during my contractions like some coach of an intense competition. I performed my athletic performance like a star until she thought I needed stretched. At that occurrence I screamed at her to stop. She calmly explained as if I were a dummy, that "it wasn't me." I shamefully countered, "It was, too! Get your fingers out of me!" As she started to explain further, I asked Luke, "Does she hear anything I say?" Luke told me to calm down, but when the midwife obeyed me, that particular pain stopped. I had enough to deal with already.

A few contractions later, at 10:05 pm, our baby was born. It was a girl! The nurses said, "She's a moose!" and took my baby away to the far corner for their emergency procedures. I listened to her cry a lonesome, frightful cry. Why wasn't she with her mother? Finally they brought our black haired daughter to us. She weighed nine pounds and fourteen ounces and was fourteen inches around the head. She was our Nyomi Shanook Munsen. Nyomi means "pleasant" and "a joy," and what a pleasant joy she is today.

One of the features of the birth plan was that we wanted to nurse our baby immediately and have some time to recoup before visitors (which I never wanted anyway, but after all the traffic in and out during the birth, family was a much welcome sight—besides, we had to show off our labor of love, even though nobody was allowed to hold her). We began to nurse our daughter, but only a few minutes into it, we were being told that we must stop nursing to be wheeled in a chair to the recovery room. But before this, family and friends could come for a quick visit. So, everyone crammed into the room for a fast viewing and left. My parents stayed and followed to the recovery room. There, nurses came in and started fretting that they needed to take and feed Nyomi sugar water. Without it, they said, she could suffer brain damage since she was a big baby and although breast milk could have taken its place, I had only fed for a few minutes. That wasn't long enough, and now they need to feed her the sugar water quickly. I told them definitely not. They became frustrated with me, and I became untrusting of anyone coming around. They sent in more reinforcements explaining the detriments of not giving her a sugar bottle, and we calmly explained how we were not giving her a bottle at all. They continued saying that it could be done with a syringe. We told them "no sugar water period. We are nursing only." It became our second labor of love to fight for our beliefs for our daughter and her health. Finally they gave up and, after pictures, my family left. Nyomi slept in my bed the whole night, and she never left the room without Luke, no matter what slight reason they had. She was in our care, and care we would.

Looking back, I see that the labor itself was not bad as others would view it, by comparison. The staff did their best to be prepared for the worst situations. And, if we ever need urgent medical assistance, then we know where to get the best possible care. I'm so grateful those doctors are there for those who need it.

I know I behaved quite ungratefully and sinfully. Love humility, meekness, and prayer would have accomplished a lot more. It would have set a better example as well. After all, I called myself a Christian at the time. Nevertheless, this was the true state of my heart during this period.

Today, I still believe pregnancy is *not* an illness and childbirth is not a procedure. In addition, every child needs a different labor and delivery for its own person. And where Luke and I started the family with God, we believe, *for us*, our birth should be with God. He can do it all better and without the stress. We are so thankful for our sweet and precious daughter.

CHAPTER 2

Malachi Edward Munsen

~ Born September 2004 ~

When we were pregnant with Malachi, we visited the independently-owned Spokane Midwives for a consultation. They granted permission for our request to put off check-ups and appointments until I was six months along or so. After Nyomi's birth, I wasn't convinced I wanted *anybody* present at the upcoming birth other than Nyomi and Luke. After all, I figured I had a midwife with Nyomi so how could another midwife be any different from them? (I found later that independent midwives—particularly lay midwives—are much more non-interventive.)

I was certain I could not have an unassisted birth legally. I thought there had to be a law against it. I started planning ways I could be gone or away to have the baby by ourselves. Or, maybe I could be so far into labor that "we didn't have time to call the midwife until too late." To prepare for our homebirth, I began to research in the library and on the internet. I came across a few unassisted childbirth websites. I couldn't believe it! It was actually legal! I researched the idea more deeply and one day brought piles of printed information home to present my idea to Luke. I had my speech all thought out, armed with the information about having the baby all by ourselves and doing our own prenatal care as well. As soon as I mentioned it, Luke was all for it! We excitedly went through the information together and prayed about it. It took loads of stress off both of us. I continued to check out books, research the web, interview midwives and listen to birth conversations until I filled my three inch ring binder with research and stories. We even bought special scissors and clamps for the cord.

It wasn't too long into pregnancy when God showed me birth would be best in water. He also showed me that I would need to squat to aid delivery. So I brought this to Luke, and he consented to my searching into water births. Subsequently, we bought a kid's pool that is six feet in diameter and twenty-five inches deep with six-inch inflatable sides that were sturdy enough to lean on, and an inflatable bottom. We found this pool at *Toys R Us* as suggested by a water birth site. With a waterbed hook-up kit, we were set!

We both needed to trust God to be our Physician, and that alone helped us to grow spiritually. We also grew together, too. I had to turn *all* my fears of "what-ifs" over to God. For a birth to happen naturally you need to get over your fears. God said he will take those for us, and He did! With our close relationship and the trust and faith required, we were able to listen and tune into Him. The fears we had to give up were peritoneum tears, excessive bleeding, the baby getting stuck, and either the baby or me dying or getting hurt.

Tearing was the biggest issue, I think. Early in pregnancy, I told Luke our baby was a boy, would look just like him at birth, and to be prepared for an eleven-pounder. So we prayed the size would not become a fear and trusted God to take care of our large baby and the passageway for it. I think that is why the tearing and the baby getting stuck were our biggest concerns.

At the time, we were living on the South Hill in Spokane in a basement apartment. We had informed the landlord of our intentions, and he was supportive. Nearing my due date we aired up the pool and practiced a dry-run of filling it up and covering it, then the cleanup and emptying it. We had it timed to see how long it would take. It ended up being quite a fast and efficiently-clean setup and take-down. I had tested my birthing position in the pool and found the inflatable sides and bottom to be extremely comfortable, and I was well supported. All this was being set up in Nyomi's bedroom. The plan was to move her bed into our room when I went into labor. We set up candles ready to be lit and the radio that would play my chosen Randy Travis' *Worship and Faith* CD while I was in labor. With the candles and soft worship music, we had our birthing atmosphere perfectly ready. My sterilized supplies were pool side and ready for use. Extra sheets and newspapers were also ready to be spread on the floor from the pool across the hallway to the bathroom in case I needed to walk back and forth. Then the wait began.

My due date came and went. Three and a half weeks past my due date, I finally started labor! We knew God did not make the body faulty. He designed labor to start when it "was time." We trusted God's timing for the full development our unique baby needed.

September 24, 2004, I awoke at one o'clock in the morning with a hard contraction. Somehow I *knew* I was in labor! I woke Luke to tell him, and we decided to give it thirty minutes to see what else would happen. A few minutes later, I was too restless and excited to stay in bed. I mentioned to Luke that it was definitely labor and I thought we needed to get Nyomi moved and the pool filled up, covered, and everything ready. I called Mandi, our friend whom we had decided to have present at the birth, so she could come over. We had decided to have her there with us since it was our first unassisted home birth and in case I needed something and didn't want Luke to leave me to get it. She could help both Luke and me. If we birthed during the day she would have helped watch the kids as well (I say kids because she has a boy almost the same age as Nyomi). I wanted Mandi because I knew she would not interfere, would stay in the background, not panic, be very helpful, quiet, encouraging during the right times, and she supported all my views so I could completely relax.

By the time Mandi arrived, I had been in labor for almost two hours. I met her at the door and helped her carry her things in. Yes, I was still in stage one. Action stopping contractions, but still stage one. We got all the kids settled in our bedroom, and the birthing equipment, supplies, candles, juice, etc. were arranged, lit, and ready. In fact, we never did turn on the lights so it was constantly dim with candlelight. It was perfect! Shortly afterward, my smile disappeared, because I now needed to concentrate on relaxing and not fighting contractions. I very soon entered the pool with Luke, and immediately I felt my body relax more. I leaned back on Luke while he held me. We prayed and I was able to doze off every once in a while. The music and candlelight were greatly appreciated. It kept everything soft. It wasn't too long before I became concerned about Luke having to stay in the pool for so long. So we got out and went into the living room. That was not a good idea! The colder air seemed to bite into my skin. I tensed up and couldn't lie down to relax. Instead, I stood in our kitchen area which overlooked the living room and the pool in Nyomi's room and proceeded to rock side to side.

I prayed God would give me strength and tell me what I needed and when. A few moments later I looked into Nyomi's room, and next to the pool stood what my heart said was my beloved Jesus! It just seemed so natural that He was there I never thought anything was unusual. It was a few seconds I watched Him stand there. He motioned gently, but definitely, towards the pool with His right arm and asked, "Are you ready?" very quietly and very calmly. I was filled with peace as my heart answered "yes." I then glanced at Luke and Mandi to see if they were seeing this, too, and when I looked back, He was gone.

I went to the birthing room saying nothing, and I spent the rest of labor in the pool. God always knows best! I needed that pool of hot water to labor in. Things got *intense,* and I knew I had entered transition. I asked Luke to talk to me. I needed to hear his love and soothing voice. I needed him and God urgently. We both praised Jesus and thanked Him between contractions. God really helped me through, and I praise God for giving me Luke who knew exactly how I needed to be talked to. Luke was my earthly rock.

At times when I didn't think I could do it anymore, I would hear the worship CD singing of my God, and I could relax more and *know* I was not alone. It wasn't long before my body had the urge to push. We had decided to not push and let my body do it on its own. Once again, God knows best! Without my help, my body would voluntarily "crunch" down. I didn't have to exhaust myself. The body my Great Physician created for me worked! How odd that we are taught otherwise! Contractions were five minutes apart at this point but hard when they came. I talked in between when desired, praised my Father in Heaven, and rested. Then the next one would come and my body would dutifully bear down, or double over.

About thirty minutes later, Mandi left to go to the bathroom, and two contractions birthed my son into my waiting hands. Amazing! What a joy to catch my own baby! At my loud exclamation, Mandi came in to find our baby boy had arrived at 5:30 in the morning! Four hours and thirty minutes of labor. It seemed so fast! We named him Malachi Edward Munsen, and he was a miniature replica of Luke: curly red hair and green eyes!

He was healthy and reddish-pink. We decided to suck out his throat anyway. However, we couldn't seem to get the aspirator in his mouth. We flicked on the light momentarily to realize that the birth sac was still intact around him! (There was a tear in the back side only). We shut the light off since it was too bright and proceeded to tear off his "veil" in the candlelight—just like opening our gift from God. We sucked out his throat to find it was unnecessary and pulled him out of the warm water into ready blankets. He was breathing perfectly, looking around, and still not crying. What a calm birth, and what a calm baby! Praise the Lord!

We then cut the cord, as it was white. Then, Luke got to hold his son for the first time. After my shower, we all settled in the living room to weigh the baby. Malachi weighed *ten pounds and three ounces*! WOW! His head measured fourteen and one-half inches around! WOW again! AND...I didn't tear one tiny bit! I later learned that squatting fully maximizes the opening of the pelvis and that is exactly what God had shown me to pass my big boy! Praise and glory to God, our Great Physician!

CHAPTER 3

Two Miracles, One for Each Day

We will now jump almost a year ahead and share a vivid miracle that took place in the year of 2005.

Year 2005 found us living in an A-frame house we had remodeled (in Mount Spokane, Mead, Washington). The original structure was fifty years old before we began to build on it. Then, our family included Luke and me, Nyomi and Malachi. Malachi was around eight months old. The A frame was about eight hundred square feet, and we were building an addition that would double our living space. On this particular day, we all loaded up in the old Ford pickup with our fifty-gallon water drum and various other water containers, to replenish our water supply. We had power, but did not have plumbing or running water.

We drove the half mile to Luke's dad's house to refill. While Luke refilled, the kids and I ventured into the garage to see the progression of the new apartment/recreation room being finished in the loft of his new double garage. Luke's step-mom Caron was working hard, and as there were no stairs, I visited from down below for a few minutes. Deciding to take a quick peek at the progress, I surveyed Malachi standing at the parked snowmobile across the thirty-foot-wide garage opposite me. He was not walking yet, but he could pull to a stand and try cruising. Figuring it safe to dash up, glance around from the ladder, then return down, I climbed up. I promptly surveyed the work and it was looking quite well. She was doing a great job!

I began to descend the ladder and had only gone a few rungs down when the ladder feet started to slip out. My mind scrambled for some way to safety, but my fingers clung to the ladder. The ladder stopped a second after it started. I froze, afraid of moving, when in slow motion I started falling. All of a sudden, I landed with a resounding thud on my posterior right on top of the ladder. As my senses were catching up I vaguely heard Malachi crying. Adrenaline shot in overload as I realized my baby was directly under me. Malachi was flat on his belly with his head under the edge of the ladder. I flew off the ladder and with one hand flung the fiberglass twenty foot extension ladder aside five feet as if it were Styrofoam. I had fallen from the second story right on top of my baby boy! The ladder edge, not the rung, was on his head when I threw it off. I thought I was hearing the last cries he would ever give, but I counted it a blessing Malachi *was* crying *and* moving.

As hard as it was to not touch him, I restrained all panic and impulses with a prayer to our Father in Heaven. Only split seconds had passed. At my calm encouragement, he started to crawl, but to my alarm, it was not only disoriented but in the wrong direction. I soothingly called to him and felt relief when his bearings reached him initiating a turnabout and straightway he crawled to me. I gently lifted him and cradled him to my chest as I examined body and limbs. All felt fine, but there was a rapidly growing bump of purplish red swirling under the skin on the top, left side of his forehead. He was no longer crying, but quiet and wanting to drop off to sleep. I held my baby tight, praying hard and keeping Malachi awake. I was anxious for Luke to return, as he had gone inside the house to the bathroom. The shock from my own fall prohibited me from standing, and Caron and Nyomi were stuck on the second floor since the ladder was down. The two of us sat and prayed.

Luke soon came out and, at the look on my face, quickly dashed over. First thing, I told him, "We need to pray." With our hands together on our blessed child, Luke beseeched our Living God, our Great Physician for immediate healing. I then recounted the events. He sat down beside me as I continued to rock our baby and gain strength to move myself. We discussed heading to the hospital, but this was fast vetoed as the bump had not only quit growing, it had shrunk! God Almighty is so very sovereign and powerful! We decided to go back home and call the nurse hotline first. If they referred us in, we would go. Therefore, Luke reset the ladder with a stopper at the bottom and brought Nyomi down and we all headed home.

We called the nurse hotline, received voicemail, and left a message. Malachi was already becoming more responsive and active, in addition to his bump continuing to recede. We continued to praise God, pray, and hover over our son. One hour after the fall, the nurse had called back and following discussions, she reported we were only dealing with a mild concussion. The instructions were to watch him at home, don't let him sleep, and if things get worse or don't improve after several hours, bring him in. We hung up and heard Malachi laugh at Nyomi as they were heartily playing.

Two hours after the fall of my one hundred forty pounds plunging from the second story on a heavy ladder, slamming the ladder's edge onto an eight-month-old baby's soft head, which could have crushed and killed him immediately—two hours afterward and our gracious, praiseworthy God restored our gift back to us one hundred percent. Not even a mark or bruise was left. Although I thought I was holding my dying baby, two hours later he was crawling, laughing, and playing normally with no signs or marks whatsoever. I say *that* miracle compares with the Red Sea! All the glory to God for my health, too, as I was healed of my soreness by that two-hour mark as well, *and*, for the peace bestowed on us to trust and allow God to show His mighty power.

All too often the hospital and doctors are relied on and depended on as the final say. We must always remember, whether we are in the hospital, home, or elsewhere, that God has the last say.

To explain the A frame floor plan, it held a balcony or loft, twelve feet long by six feet wide with an additional sixty-four square feet bedroom on each side of the balcony hallway. Against the wall in the balcony hallway were our clear storage drawers used as our dresser. This hallway between the two rooms had no railing on its edge. To access this balcony loft area we used a ladder, as we had not yet finished the addition where the stairs would be.

Sunday morning (the immediate day after our ladder miracle), I was putting away laundry upstairs and Luke and Nyomi (about twenty months old) were upstairs changing for church. After I finished putting Nyomi's clothes away and had her dressed, she was to wait in her bedroom until the hallway cleared and we could safely take her downstairs. I left the bedroom carrying the laundry basket into the hallway where Luke was in front of our dresser. The very moment I stepped out toward the edge to move around Luke, Nyomi decided to run around me. Before I could stop my step, Nyomi crashed into my outward moving hip and bounced off over the edge! As if in a dream I watched her flip over and land on her back on the floor below! Luke didn't see the initial collision, but I had immediately screamed and Luke, turning, saw Nyomi's flip and landing as well. He screamed. Nyomi instantaneously began to shriek and merely ventured to roll over.

After yesterday's ladder event, this caused great panic. I screamed again which caused Luke to scream, and when I heard Luke I thought the situation was worse than I first thought and screamed in fright *again*. So seconds had passed in the pandemonium before Luke scrambled down the ladder. When I reached the bottom of the ladder, Luke had our little twenty-month-old, curly-haired daughter in his lap, praying, soothing her tears, and angry at himself for not having built a railing. The fall had knocked the wind out of her, and it took her a few minutes to recover (us, too).

God had miraculously preserved our precious daughter for us. To explain further: standing from the loft hallway looking down, there is a seven-foot tall by three foot wide window at the wall straight ahead, floor level, with a six inch sill protruding at the bottom. Not even a three-foot by two-foot floor area was clear in front of the window. If Nyomi had fallen any more to the right, she would have split over the wooden rocking chair. If she had fallen any further forward, she would have slammed onto some large-sized hard toys. Landing any further back would have resulted in a collision with the window and sharp cornered sill, and further left stood more furniture. The way Nyomi flipped and fell landed her in the *only* space on the floor that would hold her body size.

After awhile Nyomi was entirely composed and Luke went to put her down to check for more injury. When she stood, she cried aloud as one of her legs buckled. Luke scooped her back up and we reexamined, still coming away with nothing noticeably wrong. Through Luke's prayers of faith, we settled with peace about it being shock to her body, and we trusted and leaned upon our Great Physician to heal it completely. We proceeded to church, all four of us and Luke carrying Nyomi everywhere. After church we briefly tested her leg again and found a little improvement. It didn't daunt us at all, but strengthened our reliance and trust in God as we knew He understood the problem and could heal it better than anyone. At home again that afternoon, she could not only stand, but limp around. The next day Nyomi limped as well, and Luke built the railing across the balcony. The third and following day God healed her body completely, one hundred percent!

With faith we can go to our Creator for our supplications, however small or big. If we trust and believe in His might, then we can let God out of the box we tend to hold Him in. At that time we can behold the power and miracles of His grace, mercy, and love.

I love to think on the abounding love our Father gives us. Without the sacrifice of His own Son for our salvation, we could not go to our Father and obtain peace, mercy, healings, love, or even the love that includes discipline. How backwards to think it is only love if God allows us to go any froward way we wish. To expect *God* to set rules for our own good and *Himself* turn away from them in "love" and chase us as we "experience" our next curiosity or pleasure. It's nearly blasphemous.

"The fear of the Lord is the beginning of wisdom..." [Proverbs 9:10]. Fear is the recognition of His righteous judgments and power as stated in Deuteronomy 32:39 "...I kill, and I make alive; I wound, and I heal: neither is there any that can deliver out of my hand". He has shown this in history, and He will show it vividly again soon enough. If we forget it now just because of His grace and mercy to this era, then surely "...the day of the Lord shall come as a thief in the night" [1 Thessalonians 5:2]. We must all prepare now by acknowledging our deserving punishment as rule-breakers, as sinners in every sense. Only this repentant humility can cause us to rejoice in the offered free gift of love and salvation: to accept, take, and remember the blood Christ Jesus shed and sacrificed for every one of us.

This should indeed fill our hearts with love and abundant gratitude for our renewed opportunity toward an intimate relationship with our Great Father in Heaven. This love makes it seem a small token to sacrifice our lives to further God's plan, serve and obey His commandments, and offer this joyous life and gift to others. This love helps us to rejoice when trials come. Sometimes these trials are discipline from our Father. Sometimes it is experience to be able to come alongside another and help them through and sometimes it is strictly a consequence of our own free will to walk away from God's path and do it "our way." When you come right down to it, there is never cause to grumble or murmur at God for occurrences in our lives—a particularly challenging task for anyone.

Learn to rejoice and praise Him during these times, and run to your Father crying "Thank you for loving me enough to help me stay on the path!" Learn not to worry—which is a stronghold for Satan to tempt you away and "handle things your way" rather than wait and watch God unfold His plan. Be humble and a wise learner. Search scripture diligently, apply it all to your life and pray constantly, for God knows the way through the maze of tunnels and paths. Don't start running through any door opened in a blind, grasping panic. Trust God.

CHAPTER 4

The Lies of the Fish Story

The weekend of Christmas, year 2005, found us visiting my parents. Saturday night my dad was rocking Malachi as he seemed sort of "under the weather." My mom asked me if something was wrong with his neck, as he seemed to not want to move it. I had not noticed at all! Sure enough, when I called Malachi's name, he didn't turn his head. He turned his body to see me, keeping his neck stiff. Upon further examination, we found the left side of his neck was swollen and tender to the touch. Because it was Christmas weekend, doctor offices were not open. We only had the emergency room to go to, and we knew that would be expensive. At the moment it didn't seem like an emergency. We decided to apply a few hot compresses, hoping they would relieve and draw out the suspected infection. We really had no idea what the problem could be. I thought maybe it was an overfilled lymph node, but the center point was at the front side of his throat and not under his ear where I assumed the nodes were.

Since Malachi showed no sign of discomfort besides not pivoting his neck, we hoped the fluke occurrence would go away as fast as it came. As it was late, Luke decided we should sleep that night and see how he was Sunday; perhaps we would leave early rather than stay the extra days. Our health insurance was picky and we had to go to the same doctor unless we called in for a referral. Spokane (we still lived at the A frame) had minor emergencies/ urgent care facilities open, so we could go home and be referred on the way.

Sunday morning found no improvement for our son. He now lazed around lethargically. But there was no cold or fever, only the swollen neck which had grown. Sunday was Christmas Eve and everything was closed as well as on Monday. However, the growth never stopped. What started as barely noticeable rapidly became swollen out to his ear. We packed our things and went home that Sunday morning. We could better treat his neck at home where my herbs, were as well as go to our Great Physician as often as desired without being spectacles. Our silent pleas of comfort, wisdom, and care for Malachi sustained us on the way home. Once back home we, as a family, went before God with our supplications. I then picked out some herbs and made some strong tea. I held some hot compresses onto the swelling before soaking a folded paper towel in the tea, applying it to his neck, covered with saran wrap, and wrapping his neck with an ace bandage. After we unpacked, I removed the wrapping. I then applied a garlic poultice for sixty seconds (as garlic can burn and blister skin) before wrapping in fresh tea for the early afternoon. Luke called our insurance for a referral and permission to go to the urgent care on Monday.

Malachi was moving around fine and being active again, although not to normal standards. Monday morning found us waiting at opening hours at the Urgent Care Clinic. We weren't sure what to expect. We suspected infection, but there was no fever. We finally saw the doctor and he immediately referred to the swollen bump as "the size of three golf balls!" He wasn't sure what it was caused from, but explained the abscess needed to be drained. He sent us to a different local hospital—as it was more oriented to children—and said he would personally call the doctor and refer us straight through so we wouldn't have to wait.

When we arrived, they took us right in to another waiting room. The doctor finally showed up and confirmed the "three golf-ball-sized abscess." They didn't know what had occurred, but their procedure required Malachi to go to surgery so they could slit it open and place in a tube for draining. He would have to remain hospitalized overnight. I wasn't too excited, but we were there now, and we had God with us as we still felt this needed to happen. I asked if I could be in the room with him, but they said no as he would "be out" anyway. Eventually they wheeled him off, and Luke made plans to take Nyomi home overnight while I remained with Malachi. We praised God for keeping him safe. The doctor and nurses enjoyed Malachi's stay so much that the doctor himself called to check on Malachi's progress two days after we returned home.

Perhaps a week passed as we kept the dressings on his neck clean. Then, although the incision was healed over, the incision itself started turning white and puffing back out (only the incision). Knowing the only thing medical help would do is drain the pocket, we didn't want to pay the costly expense when we could induce healing ourselves by patience, compresses, and prayer. So we laid our hands on Malachi and asked for our Father's wisdom and help. Afterward, we began a *long* road of compresses. Although I cannot recall every herb I used, I do remember Echinacea, eucalyptus, and garlic were the herbs we used most (as those are great for boils, abscesses and other skin problems, and they are what we had on hand). Merely a few days of diligence resulted in the infection drawing further and further out to the skin to create a taut white volcano directly under and only where the surgery incision was made. When it seemed to peak, we would double the compresses and poultices. Sure enough, when cleaning the bandages there would be an eruption of green yellow goo all over the bandage. The compresses following would continue to draw out the goo until, even though still applied, the skin healed over normally. Malachi would get a few weeks free from any bandaging around his neck before it would come back. We would see the first signs of whiteness that preceded the build up and swelling and once again we would begin the process of prayer, making teas, compresses, and wraps. We were very disheartened at times because it would go away and come back so much.

After months of this we became weak in our trust in God alone and again went to a doctor. From there we were referred to a pediatrician. After consulting and prodding, he began to tell us of a sebaceous gland in the neck and how infection had taken residence. It didn't sound too terrible, and we were relieved to finally find someone who seemed confident in his answer and had had prior experience with this.

AND THEN...

We hear "the gland is formed in the womb...it is actually the amphibian stage of development, and this gland was his gills. Normally, what happens is that the gills close off and the body absorbs this gland. However, occasionally, as in this case, the gland is not absorbed. An infection takes place, and the next step is to remove this gland ..."

We dumfoundedly asked, "As in surgery?"

He continued to drone on about surgery and how it is paramount to prevent further complication.

Okay, the gill thing seemed absolutely ludicrous, but feeling as if we were in enemy territory and wanting to get the family out safely and together, we agreed to set a surgery date. Once set and we were at home, we prayed hard for a way out. Looking back, I wonder why we didn't just cancel, but after six months of using home remedies and discussing the possibility of Malachi having to treat this his whole life, we ran out of strength. Why? Because we began to rely on our *own* strength and our prowess and ingenuity in healing it. We forgot the cruciality of our dependence upon God. But through prayer God helped us to turn our control to Him. We were not going to consent to the surgery, especially under an ignorant doctor who was all too ready to put our child under the knife, on his neck, to search for a missing gill! Thankfully, God healed Malachi's neck temporarily. We promptly called and cancelled the appointment, and soon the doctor called back to ask why. We could *honestly* tell him that it was healed, and we didn't want to do it anymore. He went along with it and said we could reschedule if needed and he would leave a note that we could reset a date without consultation if it came back again.

We enjoyed the healing reprieve for a month or so, praising our Father in Heaven. But the problem returned. Compresses this time didn't seem to help as they had before. Polluted with the thoughts of gills and the "worse" complications as were told us, we became desperate, as the only thing that seemed to hang before us was surgery. We half decided to do it as we felt a suffocating atmosphere of "countdown." On our knees, together, we sought after our Holy Father, our Creator and Designer for help. Very soon Malachi fell ill. His neck was wrapped, his face and skin white (almost transparent), his countenance weak and lifeless, and he had a high fever. Rapidly, things got worse. All night we both sat up and rocked our son who was now completely inactive and hardly responding due to the intense fever. We monitored his fever every few minutes and watched it continue to get worse until it read 104.5 degrees Fahrenheit in his armpit! Three times in a row it read this. Knowing this could be dangerous, it was a miracle that God gave us the assurance to hold off and not panic. We knew fever was the body's way of killing off infections and also knew God was in control. If our son was to be with us, it was to be by God's plan and will. The night was full of reverent and humble praises and thanks to God for His ability to conquer the illness and make everything turn out according to His plan. That was our biggest comfort—to know it would be okay if we didn't understand because our very Living God *did* understand. While we rocked our son, we made plans for a tepid bath if the temperature raised *AT ALL*! It never did. It continued for a total of five minutes at that temperature, and God began to restore our son. Just as steadily as it climbed, it receded to 101 degrees Fahrenheit. After a few more hours at that steady reading we all went to bed trusting our patient to God's holy care. We all slept soundly—full of peace and praise.

Upon waking mid-morning, we rechecked Malachi's temperature and found it completely normal save for the incisions still present! We are so undeserving of such mercy. However, we rejoiced exceedingly to witness God's mighty hand in this occurrence. He sustained Malachi and us during this hard tribulation. Malachi's body was not failing but performing the very way it was created to. In our final desperation, a fever was allowed by our merciful Physician. Even though it was exceedingly high, it was never left unattended by God. He used it to show how His design *works* and prove the intelligence behind the design. He was a little weak from the day before, but with a few naps, the following day found him back one hundred percent! *Never again did or has his neck ever flared up*!

Isaiah 55:8 says "For my thoughts are not your thoughts, neither are your ways my ways, saith the Lord."

John 1:3 says "all things were made by Him; and without Him was not anything made that was made".

The scar on Malachi's neck is a reminder to everyone, including Malachi and us, of the majestic glory of our Father in Heaven, the only true God. I hope the scar never disappears, for it repeatedly shows God's divine glory and power.

Again, Deuteronomy 32:39 "...I kill, and I make alive; I wound, and I heal: neither is there any that can deliver out of my hand." As Job says, naked we came into this world and naked we will go out. Everything we have is God's: our health, our possessions, our life, our success, and our failures. What we do have, God can blow on and—POOF—it can be gone.

We do not need another man, institution, organization, book, CD or DVD to tell us what the Word says. We know Jesus gifted us the Holy Spirit to teach us because 1 John 2:27 informs that the anointing we receive from the Holy Ghost abides in us and "ye need not that any man teach you" because the Anointing will teach us and it *is* truth and *not* lies. 2 Peter 1:20-21 imparts, "Knowing this first, that no prophecy of the scripture is of any private interpretation. For the Prophecy came not in old time by the will of man: but holy men of God spoke *as they were moved* by the Holy Ghost." And for that reason, all scripture "is profitable for doctrine, for reproof, for correction, for instruction in righteousness" (2 Timothy 3:16).

Follow and seek after our Creator. Follow His principles set before you in the *Holy Bible* and add no book alongside it. Study the Word, depend upon God and cling to His gift for you, His only begotten Son: the way, the truth, the life. Without Jesus Christ and His death on the cross, we could not go before our Heavenly Father for any supplications of healing, protection, blessings, or anything else.

CHAPTER 5

Courage James Munsen

~ Born July 2006 ~

My pregnancy and childbirth with Courage is one I had pushed aside in memory for a long time thinking it was unimportant just because it was hard and more delicate than the others. But I want to record what little I do remember since there is *always* a lesson to remember.

This particular time in my life saw me well "under construction." God was cleansing and converting my heart. We were not reading His Word steadily at this point in our lives, but God spoke mightily and unlocked what *was* read. I was learning what it meant to be a woman of the house under my God-given authority. I had at least fifteen years of esteemed notoriety in sports to break from. I had a matriarchal culture to break from. I had years upon years of recognition, pride, and control to break from. I had myself to break from.

I remember the state medals and front page news clippings and numerous plaques of achievements and honors bestowed upon me year after year. Luke had tall trophies of memorabilia from snow skiing competitions and boxing competitions and plaques as well.

I thought it would be incredibly neat for the children to grow up and see a part of their parents' past and accomplishments. So, we planned for the upstairs hallway in the new addition we built as our own "hall of fame." We thought to raise-up *ourselves* in our children's eyes. How incredibly prideful! Luke had before told me he didn't want his trophies up anywhere and wanted to throw them away as they embarrassed him when seen. But I was very controlling and wouldn't honor my husband and follow his wisdom. I told him "no way," the kids would love to see the great things their daddy did just as we enjoy to look back upon pictures of our parents. Therefore the hall of fame was planned for as we began building the twenty by twenty two-story addition on the back of the A frame. God allowed me to put it all up in my hard-heartedness. But it would've been easier to listen first at His promptings than to take it down later. The confusion, the battle, the irritation that comes with spiritual warfare is not worth it. I remember the struggle and indignation at the thought that I needed to remove my stardom, my "identity." I later agreed with Luke that we need to break from the past and uphold Christ's example as our future. To display the paraphernalia was prideful. So, I took pictures of all the trophies and put them in our scrapbook.

It took awhile to surrender as I didn't put on the whole armor of God (Ephesians 6:11) and as a result, I never told Satan to back off. I allowed him to confuse me and tell me how important I was— that I could be both a helpmeet and athletic at the same time. I don't have anything against being athletic, but I was upholding my athleticism as valuable. I wasn't parading around telling every one of my accomplishments or being arrogant. However, we must acknowledge inner pride. This pride in my heart would tell my spirit that I deserved recognition from my husband, that I was equal. "Every one that is proud in heart *is* an abomination to the Lord:

though hand *join* in hand, he shall not be unpunished" (Proverbs 16:5). It mocked the very submission Christ showed as an example. It is not of God. Ephesians 5:22-24 and 33 tell wives to "submit yourselves unto your own husbands, as unto the Lord. For the husband is the head of the wife, even as Christ is the head of the church: and he is the savior of the body. Therefore as the church is subject unto Christ, so *let* the wives be to their own husband in *every thing*" and to make sure you "reverence" your husband. Jesus Christ shows us the perfect example of following His authority with obedience, submission, and complete contentment. Yes, some longsuffering too, but he never had to have the last say, nor did he attach conditions to the command. To think we deserve an equal say and voting prestige in the matter is to not follow in Christ's footsteps.

The more I began to search for who I was supposed to be to God, the more exciting my role became. I had to become submissive and see from God's eyes the purpose and fulfillment in being a housewife who loves my husband and children, who is discreet, chaste, keeper of the home (a homemaker), good, *obedient to my husband* so the word of God be *not blasphemed* (Titus 2:4-5) and a helper appropriate for *my* beloved groom (Genesis 2:18). Praise the Lord for His longsuffering and patience. Our identity in the world is vain and fickle, but my identity now, in the Word, with Jesus Christ and the Holy Ghost in me, is free and peaceful, steadfast, and secure (as long as I continue in the Word and follow my Perfect Example).

Sometimes, the conversion of the heart feels painful, as if you're being scraped clean. The pain resides in our wrestling with God. We hurt ourselves and can cause others to stumble during this gray area of ignoring our Father. I very much rejoice in the "surgery" that my heart underwent, as it was probably one of the most intensive changes that so needed to happen. Those clippings and photos are removed today because I am free of my old self and don't want those examples around anymore. I especially don't want the kids to see them, to think they are important. Reality is not what is in the world; reality is what comes after this world.

Following this, I was able to undertake the practice and habit of serving my husband, being submissive, flexible, and following him. I not only had to practice being the woman and helpmeet God wanted me to be, but I needed to conform to the wife my husband needed me to be. If I formed *my* idea of what God wanted and pushed *that* on my husband, how then, would I be *his* helpmeet? Every husband entrusts different needs to his own wife: some none, some more.

A scripture that returned to me often during this time was Deuteronomy 22:5, "the women shall not wear that which pertaineth unto a man, neither shall a man put on a women's garment for all that do so are abomination unto the Lord thy God." I discussed this with my friend, Mandi, and Luke. Mandi and I both felt led to dress more befitting the woman of God: feminine and modest.

Everything we do exemplifies our God. Each one of us will stand before Him and answer for how we represent Him, how we as wives follow and obey our husbands, for how we steward our children given to us as rewards from Him, how we steward anything He has given us, or if we are stumbling blocks to others. Luke completely supported me in this when I brought it before him to seek his advice. He affirmed that it was good, and he said he likes to see me in feminine apparel. This newfound conviction was exciting to me and served another purpose: the very act of wearing a dress/skirt molded my entire mindset to subservient helper and obeying even the smallest wishes of my husband with joy. I noticed the times I rationalized myself into wearing pants I became forthright and assertive, making my voice heard. I wasn't mean, just more disrespectful. Mandi had reported the same pattern from her submissive attitude when wearing feminine attire to her "not caring" as much when in pants. So I decided that was proof enough, and with Luke's encouragement, took every pair of pants I had and hauled them off. That left me only the skirts and dresses on hand.

To set the record straight, just because one wears a dress does *not* mean her attitude is right concerning modesty or submission, nor will a dress fix everything. Although the new attire helped to remind me of my role, once accustomed to it, I fell short in regard to keeping that constant vigilance to not step out from under my authority. In my feminine attire, I *could* become the brawling woman that so drives a man to the rooftop of his house (Proverbs 21:9). However, the clothing did what I needed it to; it gave me a start where I could plainly see the difference. I now enjoy being my husband's helpmeet and lady. Rather than force myself into the position of queen, he has lifted me up beside him and treats me as a queen in his tender care and love.

Being a lady doesn't stop there. I have noticed that the very character of a lady brings out the gentlemen's chivalry in the majority of men we encounter. Several times my daughters and I have enjoyed feeling princess-like when men see something in us and treat us differently. Even when other women are around and passing by, men stop and hold *our* doors open (not for the other women); they tip their hats, carry our bundles, and act the very part of a gentleman. This never happened before. We give God the glory for the wisdom in His Word. 1 Timothy 2:9-10 asserts "…that women adorn themselves in **modest** apparel, with shamefacedness (decency and good manners) and sobriety (moderation); not with braided hair, or gold, or pearls, or costly array (clothing); But which becometh women professing godliness with good works." Likewise "let not (your adorning) be that outward adorning of plaiting (arranging) the hair, and of wearing of gold or of putting on of apparel (fine clothing): But let it be the hidden man of the heart, in that which is not corruptible, even the ornament of a meek (gentle) and quiet spirit, which is in the sight of God is of great price (and precious)." Following God's principles has been incredibly enriching and *real*. He proves Himself over and over and over again.

So many times we are asked to obey the principles set before us and in obeying first, we understand later. We must have faith to do what is true, and we find what is true in the Bible. After all, we should be excited to seek His wisdom and with faith put it into action. He is refining us to be fit to live with Him in eternity as well as to be useful vessels sharing His kingdom here on earth. May we all be quick to follow His Word and not once denounce it with compromises and rationalizing how it couldn't mean what it says. Take the desert island challenge: if you were stranded on an island and only had the *Holy Word*, what would those scriptures say then? Unpolluted from anything, these instructions and guidelines would be your only way of life. God never changes; we just have too many distractions.

Overlapping this *same* time span, we became pregnant with our third child and were very excited. I was also very nervous because Malachi's birth was so perfect as far as births go, and I feared this one couldn't be the same. I was afraid of things going wrong. I thought "the last went so well," and my mind dwelt on the stories of multiple births being high risk and the possibilities of complications. I was sure my good birth times were up. I had immense struggles keeping God as the "frontlet between my eyes." I lacked faith. Fear is the reason I struggled so much this time with my trust and faith. I was afraid of a lot, including having to go to the hospital again. The memories of time spent there—the tension, the disregard for your person and personal options—were the opposite of what I wanted—solitude, softness, prayer, and familiarity when I birth. I would say peace too, but I took that away from myself this time, as you will find out.

We lived at the A frame. There was no running water or finished plumbing in the house the entire time we lived there. This was particularly a cause of fear, not an excuse, but a cause that I *should* have been able to submit. We hauled our water in jugs and a drum for use. However, I knew too much time would lapse in heating up gallons of water to fill up my birth pool which needed over one hundred gallons of hot water. By the time the last ones would go in the first would be too cool. This time we were to birth without water. This was a great concern to me, as it meant no soothing heat to help with the birth pangs.

It wasn't long into the pregnancy when I began to prolapsed— not immensely, but enough. I had known someone with this issue, although it was much more severe in her case. About twenty weeks came and went, and I ruled it was not a uterine prolapse, most likely the bladder. We pored over possible reasons this could be happening—the unnecessary "PUSH!" during Nyomi's birth, the fact that both my other babies had been ten pounds in birth weight, my being too active after Malachi's birth, or a simple attack of the devil. While all these may have contributed, the ailment never became a setback until *this* pregnancy.

For the first time in my life, I became an "invalid." Oh, the anguish and hardship of having to wait and ask Luke to do menial tasks for me such as lift the water jug onto the counter or carry the toddler. I was at peace that our baby was okay, but I was struggling with the turmoil of not being independent, of having to depend upon my husband. This brought on a new necessity of thanking him more often and being patient. I believe with all my heart God blessed me with that infirmity as a teaching aid. You see, at this time, I still had not taken down those plaques. I could not separate myself from them. I had convinced myself that those medals and such didn't have a hold on me. "I never even look at them!" I would tell myself.

As the pregnancy went on, so did my wrestling, but God was with me every step of the way. I couldn't go for a walk, stay in the kitchen for a baking day, etc, without the entire afternoon or the next day being mostly bedridden. Special precautions and rules of rest had to be implemented an entire full day before an event such as a reunion, even though I would go and just sit and visit. I would have to *pray* earnestly for a reprieve, and sometimes God would bless me with a break where I felt normal again. I was beginning to look at my hall of fame with disgust. What good did those emblems do for me now? What horrible reminders of what I had been and what I was now in my invalidism, unable to do a thing without God and my husband. I would think on how *much* I could do before and how *little* I could do now.

I soon realized the lesson at hand. I was supposed to submit my life to Christ, thus submitting it to God. Accordingly, if God commissioned the woman to be submissive and obedient to her husband and to help him and give him respect and reverence, then my identity must be *in* that very command. I wanted to be who God created me to be. I repented of my foolishness and proceeded to take pictures of my emblems. We rid ourselves of all trophies and certificates and awards and instead, put those pictures in the scrapbook. I believe God was encouraging me and working in the direction I was going, as I had more frequent reprieves from the prolapse. It didn't affect my health any other way except that I couldn't be active because the prolapse would drop. During the same time I learned to trust God's control in ways I never had to before. I would tell myself that the worst that could happen is my guts would fall out and we would go to the hospital, they would put me on bed rest, and after the baby, tie them up and it *all* was in God's hands anyway. So I learned to be content with the healthiness I still had and praise God for that.

The simple game of ping pong would have me near desperation to get home and lie down. I now understood how I had taken for granted the ability to be strong, to be athletic, to care for my family, to walk with my children, to play with my husband, to be "normal." God alone has the ability to give us gifts/talents and health and the ability to take them away. Sometimes they are taken for our benefit, sometimes we lose them due to our own free choice in decision-making, as we didn't allow God another choice. More often we just enjoy being under grace for the time being. What I want to make clear here is that we will never understand the majority of the why's in this life, so do not start blaming God for the occurrences in our lives or in those close to us. Praise him and rejoice always. It is a fearful thing to stand before the King of Kings and answer for those murmurings against Him. As Luke and I were beginning to seek God's will and asked for His wisdom, God was there to teach us. Seeing that I coveted and idolized my abilities, He turned the devil's attack into a good-thing, taking them away to show me the vanity of my heart's treasures.

As the end of my pregnancy term arrived and disappeared, it found me in the routine of resting and lying down a great deal. We knew the first signs of when to stop activities and rest to prevent the tired prolapse from drooping more. So although there was a lot of bed rest at the end, it did seem easier than the start. And by the end God guided me in the habit and love of respecting my husband for the way *he* wanted to do things, such as baking and cooking the way he prefers, and being flexible and finding joy and adventure in following his sudden decisions to do errands as a family that would take up the rest of my day. I learned the scenic route is beautiful, too, as well as appreciating the wisdom behind his motives and actions that I never realized before. I thoroughly enjoyed being a helpmeet! It is the most fulfilling purpose! And there are so many duties and multitasking and training and schooling and playing and cooking that the days were never dull.

Rest periods became a time for me to be content relaxing and enjoying life with my children. What a wonderful learning experience. Now, finding my identity in my Heavenly Father just opens the door to what is to come if I continue seeking Him. I without hesitation tossed the sports memorabilia out of my mind and heart. I had better things, such as a godly heritage to chase. At this point I didn't physically remove them from the scrapbook but they were as good as gone, because my heart had changed. Much later, when I did discard them forever, it was not hard at all, and I was only too glad to watch them go in the garbage.

I was two weeks "overdue" and still unable to surrender all the fear concerning childbirth; holding onto it like I was capable of changing the outcome myself. I was not sure what the prolapse would add to it, not sure how to deal with the labor and delivery, and not sure if God could handle it. I would give myself lip-service that it was in God's hands and trust Him to lead me through. It was lip service, because I know I never truly died to it emotionally, which is what it takes to let go of an issue. It's like handing God a platter with your prayer requests on it, and when you present it to Him, in your submitting them to His control and plan, at the last instant you grip tight and never allow Him to take your prayers so He can answer them.

Finally, the day arrived when contractions felt *different* this time. It was morning, and they came every fifteen minutes or more, never less. We went along with the day as planned and waited to see if they would pick up. The contractions continued all day, not painful, but hard and *working*. We retired that night expecting to get up during the night, but nothing new happened.

Early the next morning we awoke as the contractions had taken on more intensity. It was now painful and necessary for me to stop and relax through them. When they hit, I had to work hard at not tensing. We had everything ready for the birth and began heating some water. After yesterday's unbroken pattern of working contractions, I was hoping hard labor would begin soon to get it all done. God always knows best. I progressed and became tired. My attitude was all wrong. Although I wanted it over, the further I progressed, the tenser, and more fearful I became. Rather than thanks and praises to God for being with me I wanted to curse Eve for causing childbirth to be *so* painful. That is, up until Luke rebuked me by saying I would have done the same thing. He was so right. This curse of painful childbirth is my fault, I am no better than Eve. I, who have experienced God's merciful aid, help, and care during this very act of delivering a child, failed to bring into remembrance God's power and how I needed Him so very much. He was there and would have handled it, but I was in the way.

I kept Luke hopping from hot pan to tennis ball to more hot water to getting me a drink, and more. He was wonderful. By this time the pain was excruciating. I nearly was in hysterics as contractions brought me wave after wave of pain, and I would no longer relax. The tenseness caused more pain which caused more crying which caused the muscles to be taut which caused more pain. I could not calm down. Our baby finally dropped down, and rather than be excited, I remained distressed. I wouldn't relax to allow maximum opening, fearing *other* things would fall out too. Our baby birthed and it was as blue as could be.

We quickly turned the baby face-down, sucked his sinuses and airway clean, and began to massage his back and front to stimulate him. It seemed forever before he began to squawk and gain color. It was then we finally checked to see if it was a boy or girl. God had blessed us with another healthy baby boy. He weighed ten pounds one ounce and looked like an old man. He was crying, and I delivered the afterbirth in whole and bled minimally. In fact, I have never bled so little with any other birth. We can't thank God enough for taking such wonderful care of us. The whole labor lasted for thirty-one hours.

So often, even as adults, we want to pass blame for why things happen to us the way they do. We may even find ourselves blaming God for the way things happen. It's typical for a sinner to refuse responsibility for his actions. As a sinner, rather than look in the physical mirror to see if our hair looks right, it's important we look into the *spiritual* mirror to compare our heart with scripture. Sometimes we find our rebellion, sometimes we find the lesson at hand, other times we find we are just supposed to listen to Him as he unfolds our lives. I know, without a doubt, that the difficulties of this birth were my fault. I had the sole responsibility to let go of "my platter" of prayers so God could show His power. Jesus said "in all things, whatsoever ye shall ask in prayer, believing, ye shall receive" (Matthew 21:22). I completely misbehaved during this birth. I didn't trust my Physician. I didn't believe my Sovereign God. I rejected the Holy Comforter. Even though I was a wretched, ungrateful sinner, my Loving Father stayed with me, protected me and our baby, and ultimately healed me. In spite of my failings, God remained faithful, demonstrated unconditional love and showed His mightiness in spite of me. The prolapse that so stayed with me the entire pregnancy and was such a fear for me never hindered birth at all. And more than that, it has never come into play in the same ways again, even to this day. The experience also gave me motivation to consume more fluids, as staying hydrated created better health in this area as well (of course working all three Kegel muscles is a large part of it, too). I have been through more pregnancies, births, hard work, and athletic play, and it is to God's amazing glory and grace for my restored health. God has stayed it! What was so detrimental is a memory of warning today.

We named our baby boy "Courage James Munsen." Courage was a name Luke had loved since he met a companion on his boxing travels. Today, the name is all the more wonderful. We as God's children must take courage to follow His instructions. We must take courage to carry Him as our banner above all others. We must take courage to live the principles and allow *His* purpose for our lives to become ours, too. We must take courage to share His Light to others. And, for ironic word play, we need to take courage to become a humble servant, with courage and confidence, not in ourselves, but in our Living God. Romans 8:18 reads "for I reckon that the suffering of this present time are not worthy to be compared with the glory which shall be revealed in us." There is always a reason to rejoice!

CHAPTER 6

To Box or Not to Box?
That is the Question

Luke grew up as a boxer. By his teenage years he had several competitive fights, or bouts, in the ring. It was a sport loved not only by him, but by all around him except his mother and sister (even though they lovingly attended his bouts in support). Shortly after I met Luke in 1999, he became a professional boxer. The intense competition demanded intense training. It was a part-time job itself to complete the tasks of jogging, calisthenics, shadow boxing, watching films, and studying. But he was *at home* doing these activities. During our "off hours," we as a family pursued our garden and building. Three days a week, at 4pm, about three hours were required of him at the gym for training. The majority of the time we would go with him. This profession allowed ideal family time even though the family only consisted of the two of us for a few years. (I needed a lot of attention☺). Although there were some various "second" jobs here and there, Luke loved to box the most and did so from 1999 through 2007 as a professional athlete. He liked the physical training and the hard work, but he did not like the limelight.

He loved the competition, the money, and the spare time at home. He was very good, successful, and a local favorite. However, I witnessed at every fight that when the win was announced, he would hang his head with embarrassment. Instead of shaking people's hands with acknowledgement, he would quickly sneak back to the dressing rooms, oftentimes, not appearing until the utmost end of the event.

As we were babies in the Word, we were naïve in several ways. Luke was brought up as a Christian, but was weak and starving as far as being continually and spiritually fed by the Word. Luke did dedicate his career of boxing to our Lord though. Instead of upbeat rock music when introduced to the ring, Luke chose soft melodies of smooth hymns, and attire for himself and corner men with scriptures to glorify God. We were trying to honor God the best way we could. When Luke *was* approached by his fans he would immediately pass all glory and credit to God for the bout and his skill.

I take full blame in encouraging Luke to acknowledge his fans more courteously, thus extremely building his inner pride. I encouraged him not to give up his testimony, but to show love for the people by looking at them, shaking the hands of well-intentioned encouragers, to wave a hand at the shouts when he said "Praise Jesus." I, too, was well-intentioned. To Luke's defense though, he never did grow to enjoy the boisterous recognition or the cameras, but he did grow to be more comfortable speaking with people as he left for the dressing rooms.

By this time, Luke had several fights televised including ESPN. His most famous fight was against Vasyli Jirov, a seasoned Russian fighter. It was a close fight, but he lost the decision. This was all God's plan. However, loss or not, the publicity did its job and year 2006 brought an offer for an IBF world title fight.

During 2006, Luke had been studying God's Holy Word and instruction and often would share with me. The Holy Ghost seemed to take us on the fast track of learning. Many things were confusing as it unfolded many new principles. As you know already, this particular time was overlapping the birth of our third child, Courage (see chapter 5). It seemed things were changing as fast as the Word was being read.

All of a sudden God was convicting Luke about boxing and its aversion to biblical standards. Sure, God had been with us and Luke during his years of boxing, but it was time to leave. On the other hand, Luke had never done anything else, had no other profession and was adamant to not work an eight-hour day, punch-the-mundane-clock type of job, and, we had plans to pay off our A frame house and the twenty acres of land now that we were reaching larger money fights. Furthermore, now Luke was offered his dream: a real title fight. As the conviction was merely a discomfort and nothing more, he continued. He had a good four months of training to prepare for this fight. However, four months of learning from God did a lot, too. We weren't even studying in a daily fashion, but the Holy Spirit was teaching us anyway. As July and the fight came closer, the discomfort grew, but was chalked up to be "nerves."

Just prior to the event, Luke finally admitted that he didn't believe God wanted him to box. God gave him a love for his opponents and he no longer wanted to hurt people. Nevertheless, he was going through with this fight to secure the money (the most he had ever made before). Fight day found me at our friend's house in Idaho with our three children, including our three-week old baby boy, Courage, to watch Luke's title fight on pay-per-view. The very moment I saw Luke enter the ring I knew he had lost already. He had lost all heart for the ring. Knowing the caliber of fighter he was against, I was very scared now for Luke, praying for his life and for his old fighter instinct to return just to finish this fight. Luke never was one to quit. Either he would have to box smartly to stay away or be knocked out completely. It was an emotionally frightful day to watch him in that ring. God spared his life and his mind. Luke unanimously lost. I was crying—not for the loss, but for the turmoil and tension relieving itself, and angry I wasn't able to care for him, to help him. But God's timing of our baby's birth prevented any of it. I believe it was all planned by our Father, as I may have consoled him too much, and it might have bolstered his courage to try again. Luke returned, ashamed for the devastating loss, but welcomed in my arms. I later learned he didn't even feel he could rightly pray or call on God before the fight, as it now all seemed contradictory. He went into the fight alone and had never done that before. Luke was done boxing, he thought.

In the months following, Luke built pole buildings, but that job ended when the ground froze. He had a hard time with thoughts of returning to his familiar career of boxing. Satan won this battle. The end of December, 2006 had Luke beginning to train for the next bouts in January. Our gracious and patient Father never left Luke, and although he loved to be back exercising and training, the foreboding convictions of actually fighting in the ring grew stronger each day. After a few weeks of training he surrendered to the Holy Spirit's compelling persuasion. Praise the Lord! Luke never boxed again and resolved to stay away from the gym as he knew he was too weak with the temptation. Today, it is still a temptation—not as strong as before, but he recognizes it is still there.

It's another lesson never to forget. We must always analyze ourselves. The Holy Bible is our love letter from our Heavenly Father. It holds instruction for a righteous life and leads to an intimate relationship with Him. I say intimate because we have personally witnessed and felt the awesome events, lessons, reproofs, guidance, blessings, and miracles that God does for and with us on a daily basis.

We consistently stumble in our walk, and He is forever faithful. He is there to comfort and guide us again through the gifted scriptures, built one upon the other. They cannot be pulled out singly to justify our worldly pleasures as we *rationalize* our actions. The very word "rationalize" means that our minds find a way to support what our heart or conscience is telling us is wrong to do. How often do we read something too plain and obvious in its context, but rationalize not following it in its obvious state on the weak excuse of "that was only meant for their time." Be ever studious to guard against rationalism, as it is not of God. God will not rationalize your sins just to call you inside the gates of heaven. Thus, neither should you rationalize your disobedience or sins against the commandments and statutes provided. As you learn the principles and commandments in the Bible, be sure to follow them. Not as the modern world follows them, but as Jesus Christ followed them.

Luke also quit because we are to steward what God has given us and He gave us these bodies. "What? Knew ye not that your body is the temple of the Holy Ghost, *which* is in you, which **you have from God**, and you are not your own? For you are bought with a price: therefore glorify God in your body, and in your spirit, **which are God's**" (1 Corinthians 6:19-20). The price that was paid was the very blood and life of God's only Son, Jesus Christ, shed for you and me, for our sins and iniquities so we might have salvation and be restored to His heavenly kingdom. This is very precious and to not be taken lightly. Luke knew the punching was destructive to the body and forsook the only ability, skill, and understanding he felt he had in order to show God He was the most important.

I, by the time his last title fight came, shared his mother's opinion as far as hoping he would quit. We both attended the fights in support, and I didn't badger him about it, but I was certainly glad to be done with it. It caused a lot of roller coasters of emotions, stress, preoccupation, and mixed priorities which led to jealousy on my part. I felt jealousy because Luke loved his sport more than he loved me. But that is speaking from a fleshly point of view. From Luke's point of view, he was providing the best he could. But this obsession, as I frequently saw it, would cause him to spend extra time with his dad watching the fights on TV, and this caused heartache. You would think the time we spent together (as we were together a lot) would have been good enough. But these times, although in the same vicinity, weren't always *together*. I never shared his *full* enthusiasm for the sport. Don't get me wrong. I was in full support of his career path, but I wasn't in complete support of his off-hours preoccupation. I did understand the long hours of studying tapes of opponents, especially before a fight, but it wasn't *always* necessary. And to watch Luke run to his dad's for this sport rather than cuddle with me left me empty inside. I say cuddle because it means to me time spent *with* me and puts a box around a whole lot of possibilities of things we could do together to build our own relationship: reading, games, talking, dreaming, remembering, playing, laughing, building something, growing something, or studying something. I didn't always begrudge him his daddy time; I would encourage him to go when our relationship was right and sometimes because I felt incredibly selfish to want him to stay. The bottom line: *when I felt I was more important than his job then there wasn't much of anything that could go wrong*. But, it became a heartbreaking offense the majority of the time, toward the end of his career. I needed and wanted to be important and feel loved by my beloved husband. I now know I was very selfish-minded and should have been drawing my needs from my Heavenly Father instead. At the time though, I am certain Dad knew what I thought about Luke's spending so much time there as he would encourage Luke to spend time with his wife, but Luke is Luke.

Thank you, God, for giving him the Holy Ghost who can prove things to him! I am also thankful that he is not so easy to be persuaded, as it's also that steadfastness with which he stands for the Truth now.

The main purpose of this story is to express the importance of keeping your priorities right. Marriage will never arrive to be a *perfect* entity, though it can seem heavenly. But, it must always be worked on. Your wife should be able to feel that she is your number one love *under* God. A word of caution: one should never set up his or her spouse as an idol. Keeping your priorities right always means God first. Men, as you seek God, serve God, and obey God, do so with steadfast and unwavering faith. You must always lead. A godly king (as such you are of the tiny kingdom in your home) always cares tenderly for his subjects, making wise judgments, seeking for their protection and good. He never hands over his crown because someone disagrees. It is your duty to spiritually lead as best and honorably as you can. Gain wisdom through the scriptures. And remember to pray. Praying with your wife and family not only binds you together as a force with God against Satan's wiles, it helps your wife to feel included, one with you, loved and led.

I share this part of circumstances in regard for the future husbands, perhaps even the established husbands. In 1 Corinthians 11:3, Ephesians 5:23, and Colossians 1:18, God set out a ranking system. Your first priority is God, to study His Word and follow in the footsteps of Jesus Christ. Secondly, you are about your wife. Are you caring for her as you would care for yourself? 1 Peter 3:7 exhorts husbands to "dwell with them according to knowledge (with understanding), giving *honor* unto the wife, as unto the weaker vessel…" Ephesians 5:28-33 states "[28]So ought men to love their own wives as their own bodies. He that [loves] his wife [loves] himself. [29]For no man ever yet hateth his own flesh; but **nourishes and cherishes it**, even as the Lord the church…[31]For this cause shall a man leave his father and mother, and shall be joined unto his wife, **and they two shall be one flesh**...[33]so let every one of you so love his wife even as himself; and the wife see that she reverence her husband." Accordingly, how often do you help her put on her coat? How often do you make her comfortable in her chair before you sit down yourself? How often do you open her car door and help her in? How often do you tenderly support her emotions, her *godly* emotions? How often do you play the part of a gentleman to *your* lady? "House and riches *are* the inheritance of fathers: and a prudent wife *is from the Lord*" (Proverbs 19:14). Are you stewarding your wifely gift well? How well do you treat yourself in *regards to your wife*?

Most men aren't being taught chivalry today. Of course, most women won't accept it either, but I'm not speaking for the world. I speak for those seeking after our Lord. You and your wife need to be one, on the same team. Just like God, His Son, and the Holy Ghost are all different entities, but one because they are all of the same mind, goal, and purpose, each with their respective rank, assigned by God. Thus, they are all love. *Trinity* is a man's term. It is not in the Bible. Colossians 1:12-19 reminds us of our beloved God: "...[13]who hath delivered us from the power of darkness, and hath translated us into the kingdom of His dear Son: In whom we have redemption through His blood, even the forgiveness of sins: Who is the image of the invisible God, the first-born of every creature...And He is the head of the body, the church: who is the beginning, the first-born from the dead; that in all things He might have the pre-eminence. For it pleased the Father that in Him should all fullness dwell."

Matthew 19:16 speaks of a rich young ruler speaking to Jesus: "[16]And behold, one came and said unto Him, Good Master, what good thing shall I do, that I may have eternal life? And He said unto him, Why callest thou me good? There is none good but one, that is, God..." Here we have Jesus declaring a difference in rank between

God and Himself. Another example of the same principle is John 14:23-29, reading: "Jesus answered and said unto him, If a man love me, he will keep my words: and my Father will love him, and **we** will come unto him, and make **our** abode with him. He that loveth me not keepeth not my sayings: and the word which ye hear is not mine, but the Father's which sent me. These things have I spoken unto you, being yet present with you. But the Comforter, which is the Holy Ghost, whom the Father will send in my name, he shall teach you all things, and bring all things to your remembrance, whatsoever I have said unto you. Peace I leave with you, my peace I give unto you: not as the world giveth, give I unto you. Let not your heart be troubled, neither let it be afraid. Ye have heard how I said unto you, I go away, and come again unto you. If ye loved me, ye would rejoice, because I said, I go unto the Father: **for my Father is greater than I**…"

Luke and I are two different beings, and yet God refers to us as "one." "Therefore shall a man leave his father and his mother, and shall cleave unto his wife: and they shall *be one flesh*" (Genesis 2:24). So I suppose we can say Luke, I, and God are trying to make a "trinity," with all three of us on the same goal, the same page, and each with their proper ranking order, all abiding in each other, all "one." However, we hope that each will search the Word of God for himself on the matter, and we can maintain unity in Christ, believing on His shed blood and body.

As Luke says, husband and wife are supposed to be a team. A husband does not have to understand his wife's emotions, nor should she be ruled by them. A woman has been gifted emotions to nurture and sensitively care for and love the tender things in life in order to be the helpmeet, homemaker, and mother that God has designed her to be. It doesn't mean she can't handle a heavy workload. A woman's stamina and strong abilities need to be focused on "keeping the home" and other virtuous "Proverbs 31" assignments set before her.

As a husband you need to treat your wife with courtesy and tenderness, but firmly lead her. You are not her roommate but her best friend. Laugh with her; be closer than a brother to her. You are to spiritually lead and be accountable for the actions of your wife because you are her *head*, her authority. Like it or not, God designed it that way. As the leader, you are to teach her and the children so they can grow up in the Lord with you, so you can present her spotless before God. The latter part of 1 Peter 3:7 reads, "…as being heirs together of the grace of life; that your prayers be not hindered." The race must be run together. You may reach the finish line, but at the end God will ask you where your family is. Today you have the grace to return to your family and finish helping them along the way to the end. Some day soon that chance will no longer be. Husbands, search the scriptures, learn from the Holy Ghost, share, discuss, and build up the knowledge and wisdom of your family. Study often and live the example. You can only get as far as your weakest member.

Luke and I have thought of it this way: if this were a race or contest (Hebrews 12:1), and we had to scale an extremely steep rocky incline full of boulders on the way up, I would expect Luke to turn to help me with an outstretched arm. I know he could make it. But his own success does not meet the requirements of marriage. The prize comes when we win **together** ("…as being heirs together of the grace of life…"). Luke, being first, directs me where to put my feet, tells me which path is righteous, comes alongside me during the hardest times, holds me while I cry of exhaustion, and again takes the lead. And on my part, I follow, yes, follow, my husband as he leads, add wise counsel to the path before us, obey his foot placement decisions, thank him for his help, ask him during uncertainties, respectfully offer more suggestions, encourage him as he faces new ground, and perhaps hold him while he catches *his* breath. Together, as a team, we can follow the best path before us. Luke shouldn't run up the hill and turn around and yell at me to hurry up and do the same things he did. Nor should I go ahead and yell back at him, because it would cause severe frustration and disorder. The rules are set, and to make the most harmonious race we can, we must conform to the roles designed for each of us.

I want to make clear that the prize of eternal life comes by believing on the shed blood of Christ for our sins. That *is* an individual matter. Husbands can be saved and born again independently, as well as wives. Here, I am speaking of doctrine concerning marriage. *Together* you should be a force so "iron can sharpen iron" (Proverbs 27:17). Together you act as a little church to help each other and your family, live and stay on the path of Life.

Wives, it is also particularly important for you to form the habit of showing deference, respect, admiration, and even a high esteem for your husband. He has been commissioned by your living God to be the leader, not you. He will not make perfect decisions, nor would you. However, "Wives, submit yourselves [to] your *own* husbands, as unto the Lord. For the husband is the head of the wife....Therefore as the church is subject unto Christ, so *let* the wives be to their own husbands **in *every* thing**" (Ephesians 5:22-24). Your respect to your husband is a direct reflection of your respect to God. For if you fear God, you will not hassle your husband about his decisions. Pray and thank God for the wonderful husband you have. Find the adventure in going "the scenic route." Learn the fun of watching him puff his chest out as you praise him for his accomplishments and leadership (not with egotistical pride but with the added confidence you have in him to follow him). Have confidence and faith in God for His protection as you follow your husband. Read about Sarah following her imperfect husband and how God protected her (Genesis 12:10-20 and Genesis chapter 20). Be a meek and gentle spirit as you reverence your husband for the way he is created, and don't try to make him into another man. Follow the statutes set for you, and you can remain your husband's confidante. I have learned firsthand these enjoyments as I obey the statutes concerning my role as a wife. My husband loves and seeks my opinions concerning almost everything. In some areas he has asked me to make decisions and, others we share. But he loves to come to me because he understands I will follow even if his decision opposes mine.

It doesn't just stop there. It automatically descends the ranking line. When you are obeying your authority, your children see that cheerful compliance, and they are more apt to obey as well. When Luke and I are one and right together, then the children are right together as well. Everything in our marital relationship is reflected by our children. When we are together and support each other in the training of their character, they are more content as the rules are the same everywhere and all the time. When we disciple our precious blessings, they want to learn because they feel and see the love and want what we have. Love is the greatest motivation.

We ladies have a special duty to represent the bride of Christ to the world. The bride, prepared by the Father, follows the groom, and the groom submits to the Father. Don't show the world that the bride says "I don't have to do what you say...I have my own ideas... my own things to do..!" The glory of women *is* lowly submission. We dare not hate these words. They should be a light to us to follow Jesus Christ's example. He was submissive and obedient. We need to embrace those very characteristics which Christ shown first so we can be successful women in God's eyes. We will all leave a legacy with the next generation. The question is *what will it be*? Rebellion or submission?

CHAPTER 7

Accelerated Learning, Part I: The prelude to life-long lessons

In January, 2007, we went to Idaho to visit our friends who had recently moved to Osburn, in the Silver Valley. Both our families took the local mine tour offered to the public. Luke immediately fell in love with mining! Of all the jobs he came across, it was the first one he knew he could do, and, it was a means to quick high-paying money. Therefore, Luke wanted to move to Idaho, mine, and return in five years with the cash to buy our A frame and land debt free. After we returned home, he exuberantly said, "Let's go to Idaho!" and waited to see what I thought. I answered with a shrug, "Let's do it." We took the trip again to submit applications and look at a few homes, just for the fun of it. Three weeks later Luke took physical tests and interviews to be hired at the US Silver mine, or more locally known as the "Galena."

February seventeenth we were temporarily moved in with our friends while we searched for housing. Luke began work the nineteenth. While mining, advice from several sides kept telling us to buy a house. God had blessed our efforts to build our A-frame and do everything else by cash *only*. We had originally figured that we would rent while mining. All calls to secure a rental were disappointing—the houses were either located in a creepy place, rented out, or they wouldn't allow the number of children we had. Luke decided the only thing left was to get a loan. We didn't feel good going into it, but we figured it wouldn't be possible anyway as we had no credit history at all, we had no equity, and Luke had *just* begun his job. We were allowing the system to say no for us instead of being patient and trusting our Father in Heaven.

To our amazement, we were approved for a loan of $125,000 and we only asked for $60,000. It was too easy! We decided to follow the counsel that "everyone gets a loan for a house, no exceptions." We embarked on the journey of house-hunting and searched for houses costing around $60,000. Prices being at a peak in the real estate market, all the houses in three towns in that price range had either horrible or no foundations or were better left on the condemned list, leaving no resale value. We finally found a decent fully furnished house costing $110,000. We were hesitant due to our confusion and conscientious warnings, and we prayed for God to close this door if this house wasn't for us. We accepted the price, and closing procedures began. Finally, everything was pending upon the mortgage company's approval for the loan. Their appraisal was *not approved* for flooding reasons. We exceedingly praised the Lord for His handiwork!

At this point we never even thought of waiting for the right rental, praying about whether we were supposed to mine or much of anything else because we were "on a mission." We continued searching to buy a house with good structure. The very next house we looked at was the best in the Silver Valley for that price range. It was updated, had a strong foundation and just a few minor things needed improved upon for a quick turnaround. Luke wouldn't have the daunting work of renovation. He had quickly discovered that mining didn't leave the extra time for renovating a house and decided that a more expensive home would be permissible for the trade off of him being able to spend a few hours with the family everyday. The purchase went quickly and we bought a well-maintained five bedroom, 2068-square-foot home at 806 Fir Street, in Mullan, ID for $129,000. Sellers paid all closing costs, bought our interest rate down, paid our first month's expenses, and left us a new ping pong table. Everything dealing with the house including house insurance and property tax was being handled by the escrow account. Our total mortgage/escrow payment was $900 per month. We were gambling upon the future, because we did not know what lay ahead of us. We put the bondage of over $1,000 in living expenses on our family.

On the other hand, we were now excited for new reasons. This spare time afforded us plenty of time to study the Bible. Ultimately, the move became our training ground for several lessons. And we began to *really* be acquainted with our Father.

Shortly after we moved into our new home, several accidents/ health issues began afflicting Luke—from rocks and boulders falling on him to a rock chunk lodging itself in his eyeball. In fact, that rock was still stuck in the white of his eye when he arrived at the hospital. The eye specialist never expected Luke to fully recover. We just praised God that he *had* an eye and could see *at all*.

It was quite weird to get a call that night, after the kids were in bed, from the mine safety guy. He told me Luke had had an accident, and he was on the way to the hospital with him. I, thinking of ambulances and making flash plans of food items and babysitting that needed prepared and wondering who to call to watch the brood, calmly asked if Luke "was dead." Immediately there came a loud affirmation of "NO! No! A piece of rock flew into his eye and he needs to have it removed." It didn't take me long to know *Who* was in control and how I needed to dedicate my husband to Him, as the dangers exhibited in mining in the first month could drive a wife to be contentious with fear. Today, Luke can see 20-20, a long way from barely seeing a blur. We pass all glory and credit to our Great Physician.

The main ailment was MRSA (pronounced mersăh), meaning Methicillin-Resistant Staphylococcus Aureus, a specific antibiotic-resistant staph infection. It was beginning its spreading epidemic through the mine. When Luke contracted MRSA, it took us, especially Luke, through some hard trials, as it lasted about nine months. There were very strict rules about washing clothes, showering, and personal activities. I had to strongly disinfect everything on a daily basis. We lived these nine months with the contagious infection, but God mercifully preserved the children and me. There was a short incident when Courage contracted MRSA with a few bumps on his knee, but God healed him quickly and from then on we were completely protected. Even through the birth of our fourth child, Kind Providence protected our newborn daughter. Through the episode with Courage, it became quite apparent how Luke was not reaching full recovery due to remaining at the mine. As God could heal in spite of conditions, I think this lesson served other purposes as well, as you will see further on in the chapters.

It was April when we were planning and preparing for our fourth precious child from God. We continued our supplications for Luke's healing from MRSA so he could help during childbirth if I needed him, and also hold his new child. For two weeks Luke was clear of outbreaks! We deep cleaned and disinfected *everything*. We even shampooed the carpet. We were so excited! However, Luke developed another outbreak. Before, the MRSA had been on his leg or elbow, and he wore long john shirts and full long john pants threaded with colloidal silver. The infection couldn't pass through the clothes because the silver killed any infections and bacteria before it could pass through. Thus he was relatively safe and non-contagious. Nevertheless, the MRSA came back and this time on his *hands*! Wow! This was *most* unfortunate, as with infected hands, it changed everything. God would have to be my midwife Himself as Luke could no longer help.

We had a separate room set up for my water birth and only I was allowed in it because I had everything sterilized before it went in. God is so great! He not only kept the family safe and free from harm, He allowed me peace and *much* excitement at birthing "by myself." If Luke was to come in, there were procedures of fresh clean clothes, washed hands, and sterile gloves.

CHAPTER 8

Prudence Evelyn Munsen

~ Born May 2008 ~

P rudence, our fourth child, third unassisted home birth, was born May 3, 2008 at 7:30 pm. I had the most fun during this pregnancy as I made newborn and three-month size dresses. I crocheted a boy and girl set each of bunting travel suits with matching blankets, car seat covers, and other blankets. We made a log crib specific to our needs and sewed a boy and girl set of bedding, quilts, and decorations for the crib. We enjoyed a healthy pregnancy under God's guidance and protection, so I could be both fit and active as desired right up to and through the labor. All the blessing, miracles, and glory belong solely to God, who is the Author of life.

My third pregnancy was sort of delicate. Through it I couldn't be active without adverse effects. Besides the lessons I was learning, I had never lost all the weight gained from previous pregnancies and was not in the fittest of shape. After this I was determined to get in and stay in shape before our next pregnancy. I made a point to exercise even if it was merely a walk or calisthenics at home. Our diet was of natural and organic foods and void of grease, junk food, processed foods, white and brown sugar, white flour, and unhealthy fats. Our food intake was consumed in balanced moderation and made from scratch when at home. I did fine-tune my consumption amounts to better match my activity at hand and strove to drink more fluids. In the end, August resulted in my being finished nursing, back to pre-pregnancy weight before my first-born and in active healthy shape. Well, August also proved a blessing as God rewarded us with another pregnancy! Yay! I felt ready. What a joy this pregnancy was. God healed my infirmities of the previous ones and again guided me through prenatal care. Thus with our fourth child, as was the first and second, we reaped a healthy active nine months of pregnancy.

My due date, or rather the forty week mark, was May 1, 2008. At thirty-seven weeks, April 10th and 11th, Prudence had dropped immensely and the 14th and 15th were days full of hard Braxton Hicks. They came whether I was moving or sitting. I knew I wasn't in labor but we decided to start a walking regimen to hopefully prevent going too far overdue. So, five out of seven days, either I or the whole family would power walk a .6 mile loop down, around, and back up our hill. I felt quite strong doing this and praise the Lord for it. After the baby had dropped the majority of family and friends assured me that I wouldn't last over two weeks, putting labor no later than April 27th. Some were certain I wouldn't last the weekend. But I knew God had His schedule, and these "occurrences" were nothing more than interesting and fun things to journal. My guess was around May 9th and perhaps my dad's birthday, May 13th.

So, we have the baby dropping Friday, and the following Monday and Tuesday as big contraction days. The following Saturday marked a whole day of noticeably hard contractions accompanied by constant backache and pain all day. We knew that none of it was "labor", but just practice and progress. We were very thankful, for it meant less time when labor did finally start! The next week brought normal contraction activity, daily walks, and lots of hormones. The 26th, Saturday, Luke and I played Frisbee and ping pong with friends. The funny thing was—not one contraction occurred all weekend! So we settled in for two or three weeks longer.

Monday, at 39 ½ weeks gestation, was quite an exciting day. It started as a normal day with cervical contractions mingled with Braxton Hicks. After I put the family to bed at 8:30 pm, I began spotting. This had never happened with the other pregnancies, but through previous research I had learned it could, on average, be hours to a few days for labor to begin and not the weeks that we were planning. Excitement found me calling my friend, Mandi, and she confirmed that when the blood shown for her, it was never more than a few hours before labor began. Knowing my body I settled in for a hope of two more days to meet our newest member. However, I was ultimately trusting and thanking God for His timing and scheduling of labor, as He knows the baby's progress of development and growth and when it is best for the family. At this time, all the children and I were sick with a cough so I sent a prayer that the baby would not be born until everyone was healthy and done with the coughing. (We were healed and healthy two days later.) What a peace to know God as our Physician and that we are in His control no matter my flighty hopes, excitement, and wishes. It truly is security!

Sure enough, no labor Monday and Tuesday, and Wednesday resulted in quieter baby movements and more show. Everything else remained calm, peaceful, and normal. Thursday marked nothing more than lots of baby movement and activity and the forty week mark. Friday was another day of fun fullness as our baby vigorously moved all day and night.

I was looking forward to Saturday as it was our planned weekend to go grocery shopping for the following month. And what's more, Luke was taking all three of the children with him and I got to have the whole day to myself! How blessedly weird! We had already discussed labor in case it should start or happen in his absence and we were both at peace, and confident in our Heavenly Creator. There was no fear, as God does not give us a spirit of fear, and we trusted Him and His perfect love. Secretly, I had petitioned to God that I would labor and deliver while they were gone as the peace seemed wonderful. Well, plans almost changed.

It was 3:00 am early Saturday morning when I lay in bed awaiting sleep. I enjoyed the always "could be last pregnant baby movements." I soon felt a little belly hug. I was thanking God for my progression when a muffled "pop" sounded, and a tiny punch-like feeling at the same time. Having no prior experience with this, I thought "that was a weird thing for the baby to do." Then, I realized this was my bag of waters breaking! This "pop" had occurred at 5:00 am. As I lay there, fifteen minutes later brought a slow wave of strong back pain. Five-thirty found another, but it ended there. At 6:00 am I decided to get up.

I was happy as I made my bed. I wanted it to look nice and be ready for my new daughter and me to take a nap in later. I didn't actually *know* it was a girl, even though I had began pregnancy with a prayer for a girl, but the last two nights, movements had me talking to my Prudence. So Saturday morning I did make my bed pretty for my Prudence and all the cribs, car seats, and clothes were decorated and ready in their girl attire. I figured it wouldn't be hard to change them later if God gave us a boy.

In the solitude of early morning silence (everyone else was sleeping), I did the dishes, dusted, and made breakfast. I brought out my Moses Basket and readied it for her to sleep in the living room. She was to sleep in bed with us at night. I moved her other basket to its proper location in the living room. It held convenient items such as diapers, wipes, burp cloths, spare clothes/blankets, powder, garlic oil, tea tree oil, hand sanitizer, and her little hat. During all this I was having frequent water loss and intermittent belly hugs. After all the quiet work was done, I filled up the pitcher of water in the fridge, took off the filter from the faucet (to run hot water into the pool to birth in) and readied pots on the stove for boiling more hot water all just in case labor should begin. I then turned on the heater in the birth room and, to finish my tasks, folded laundry for the kids to put away when they woke up. When Luke awoke, I filled him in, and he decided to leave as soon as breakfast was over to get our shopping done sooner than later since I wasn't in labor yet.

Alone, I quite enjoyed myself as I rested first before taking a walk. At 11:30 am I ventured outside to start my yard work of raking leaves. By 10:30 that morning I had already drunk twice what I normally drank in a whole day. It was important to keep up on fluids to maintain my energy and to maintain the proper environment for the baby. Contractions hardened while raking. They didn't affect talking at all; it just made walking difficult.

Mandi called, and I recounted everything to her as we shared experiences of labor and birth. All the new experiences for me, she had had in her pregnancies and births, so it made it more exciting to learn of these things in more detail. After that phone call, I made myself two grilled cheese sandwiches, since bread and cheese were the only remaining foods we had besides split peas.

Following lunch, I finished raking the yard. During this raking session I took the phone with me to time the contractions out of curiosity. They weren't *hard*, but they came every two to three minutes while raking. When I stopped, they were four to five minutes apart. It was about 2:00 pm at this new phase, and I *knew* we were to have a baby before the day's end. Soon, every two to three minutes found me swaying back and forth and rubbing the sides and underneath of my belly through contractions, praising my Lord for His help with progression and the time I had to do this on my own. When a contraction decreased, I would rake until the next one. I finally finished raking and decided I should fill the pool up since contractions were only getting harder. I briefly called Mandi to share the updates. I then used up all the hot water in filling the pool before the pots were ready. I had three pots (an XL, L, and M) full of water boiling, and it took four cycles of carrying them all downstairs to the birthing room to get the water hot enough to stay hot (I kept it covered with a doubled tarp) and the pool half full. Although I started filling the pool with a doubt that I was too early, after the first cycle of boiling water a contraction came that wiped all smiles off my face. Without a doubt we would be meeting our baby soon.

Each new cycle of water gave me fifteen minutes to lie down, rest, and store energy for the birth before I had to unload the pots and start the next cycle. I was so thankful the entire time to be on my own. Everything around me, everything within me was completely peaceful and calm: nobody to panic, nothing to panic about. I had, and could feel, a hedge and shield of protection about me. I can compare it to dolphins birthing. When one is about to give birth, pods from all around join and remain side by side creating this huge, unified, formidable force of protection that looks like one big organism/force. Others left on the outside of this band, with the mother in center, then keep watch and protect the outskirts. All this is done in a specific spot over white sand and to safely protect the vulnerable mother as she brings her baby into the world. How is this similar? I have a specific birth spot for its specific reasons, and I have a Shield of Protection surrounding me and my property, and a band of angels to secure my location; all this to safely bring *our* gift into the world.

With yard and pool done, I tried to sit, but it was too uncomfortable and I felt closed in and wanted to go outside. I vaguely wondered how many neighbors were watching as I walked up and down our street. Every two minutes, like clockwork, brought me another *intense* contraction that burned all the way around, from my lungs to my thighs, and rubbing was no longer helpful, but something to do as I praised my Father in Heaven for the progress and for giving me strength, as well as the solitude. Some contractions would practically bring on a sob or tears as they were so very intense already. Mandi called to check my progress and we delighted in everything together. It really enhanced the event to be able to share the excitement with her. It was around 5:00 pm when Luke came home, so we ended the phone call and I updated Luke before he started hauling in and putting away the groceries. Some neighbors came to visit when they saw me out as they arrived home and were all very excited.

Perhaps an hour later I was still walking back and forth now accompanied by my two oldest children at times. Contractions were now of the sobbing sort every time. There was no sobbing or crying, just that intense pain *feeling* on the inside that about doubled you over. I was hoping this was transition and I could pass it on the road. A few moments later, all I wanted was the pool. So I brought the kids inside and Luke escorted me down the stairs. As our hot water heater had had sufficient time to reheat, Luke was going to finish filling the pool. When I arrived pool side and another contraction started, I jumped in for relief and immediately the contraction ended. I had quite the nice break as they spaced further apart. How much I'm not sure, as there were no clocks or phones by which to tell. But when they came they were bearable now.

Luke briefly appeared to bring me juice and my walkie-talkie in case I needed him. I started a CD of jazz/saxophone music only. I had candles ready, but wanted all the lights on this time, and I finally sat back to relax, rest, and dose in-between contractions. Luke appeared again and sat in the room with me for five or ten minutes while we visited before leaving to finish the grocery organizing and tend to the family. Contractions suddenly came faster and closer together. I still had no urge to push yet!

A few contractions later and I knew birth was imminent. At the very first sign of another coming, before the pain even started, God told me, "Here it comes, this one is bringing the head." I had just enough time to exhale and relax my whole body. Although it was all quietness before, it changed quickly, as I gave a guttural howl. I heard Luke give some last instructions to the children as they gathered at the top of the stairs, then he came bounding down the stairs. I was amazed I was that loud!

There seemed to be quite a lot of time on hand. I waited, wondering if another contraction was *ever* going to come. Luke stood at the doorway, new sterilized gloves on, still watching as finally the contraction came. With baby's movements, it took a few seconds to dislodge a shoulder before the final relieving whoosh as the baby slid completely out. I looked in the clear water and thought how big my baby seemed, and saw her mouth "guppying." As I scooped baby out, I glanced to see before announcing "IT'S A GIRL!" We were so excited! She made one "hello" holler and immediately quieted. She lay in my arms content as can be, mucous free, breathing, clean, her back covered in vernix, and dark red hair. She was beautiful!

My wonderful husband, who did everything I needed him to and was on-call for anything more, handed me a towel to wrap our daughter in. That pushing urge I was waiting for, never did come. God completely helped this baby arrive on His own. God, our Physician, gave me protection, peace, clarity of mind and spirit, strength, and breaks whenever I needed them. All praise and glory to Him, whom we would *never* do this without!

With Prudence Evelyn in my arms, I walked to the bathroom, still not bleeding, and was amazed to feel the placenta moving down already. Luke bustled around preparing a place for me to sit upstairs, getting me a robe, getting a dry and clean towel to re-wrap Prudence in, and helping me to hold Prudence while I cut her cord. We briefly glanced over the placenta to notice it didn't look whole, but we agreed that we were trusting God in this matter anyway and left it to relieve the children's questions and excitement. I sat and showed off the baby until Luke came and led us all in a prayer of thanks. He then set off again busily getting our bathtub ready, getting the kids their dinner, putting away the groceries, and setting up the scale to weigh her on.

All I did was sit and nurse our new baby. I noticed I was bleeding more than what was normal. I told Luke and we prayed. I also noticed I was not having after-birth pains while nursing like I should have been, as this is a sign of the uterus clamping down to its original size. We entrusted it to our Heavenly Father, and I called Mandi to quickly tell her of the good news. Luke weighed our daughter, and to our amazement, she was only seven pounds! All three other babies were ten pounds. She measured twenty inches and thirteen inches around her head.

We had "Shepherd's Purse" (an herbal tincture), so I could have taken it to stop the bleeding but I felt the bleeding was for a reason and wanted to work with it for now so I could tell when the root problem was fixed. In the bathroom I massaged my uterus; not feeling like it was an emergency yet. If any fear tried to creep in I would confess it to God and submit to His knowledge and care thus avoiding any feelings but peace and faith. A few minutes later, I wrapped Prudence in her clean towel and set her on her cushion on the floor, as I felt a prompting at this time to massage as hard as I could and hold nothing back.

With a prayer of thanks that I wasn't alone, that we had the Best Physician on hand, I started to massage with my fists and not forty seconds later passed the rest of the placenta. Immediately the bleeding stopped and I could feel my uterus begin to evenly cramp and return to its regular size. With praise and a rejoicing prayer of thanks I *knew* things were all right now.

With everything normal, I dressed Prudence and put her in her basket to sleep. Luke brought me dinner and more fluids (he had kept me replenished in fluids and ice cubes the whole time). After dinner, we cleaned up and finally got to bed at 11:30 pm with our new little blessing beside me. Again, the glory, confidence, thanks, and *all*, goes to God, my Father and Creator in Heaven!

CHAPTER 9

The Commandments

Years ago we studied the Ten Commandments. These and the rest of His written love letter, the Bible, act as a safety fence. If we choose to stay behind this fence, we are protected, safe, secure, and blessed. Thankfully, we are no longer saved by them, but they still remain as important "house rules". The following are the scriptural Ten Commandments and a few thoughts concerning each:

1. *"Thou shalt have no other gods before me"* (Exodus 20:3). This means money, family, spouse, toys, houses, land, dreams, conveniences, romance and the list goes on and on. Whatever you put before God is a god to you.

2. *"Thou shalt not make unto thee any graven image, or any likeness of anything that is in heaven above, or that is in the earth beneath, or that is in the water under the earth. Thou shalt not bow down thyself to them, nor serve them: for I the Lord thy God am a jealous God, visiting the iniquity of the*

fathers upon the children unto the third and fourth generations of them that hate me; and showing mercy unto thousands of them that love me, and keep my commandments." (Exodus 20:4-6). In today's age, not everyone makes things. So perhaps it would be fair to say you shall not make/take/buy/bring any image into your home. We believe pictures and figurines of what God created are distractions and distortions from the truth. We have personally seen how these decorations/images have taken the place of God, causing them to look to their "idol" for safety and security instead. We choose to not have any on our clothing, dishes, or in our home decorations. We found that when we removed the decorations, it made things simple. With the distractions and clutter gone, we were left focusing on the Word. We even removed the family photos from the wall and replaced them with scriptures instead. We do not need help remembering family, just as missionaries do not need to hang a photo of Africa on their wall, if God calls them there. However, we do need help knowing and remembering God and His wondrous ways, to rightly serve Him. He did say to write those on our gates and door posts (not to create pictures of them).

Deuteronomy 4:15-19 warns that "ye take good heed unto yourselves; for ye saw no manner of similitude on the day that the Lord spake unto you in Horeb out of the midst of the fire: Lest ye corrupt yourselves and make you a graven image, the representation of any figure, the likeness of male or female, the likeness of any beast that is on the earth, the likeness of any winged fowl that flieth in the air, the likeness of any thing that creepeth on the ground, the likeness of any fish that is in the waters beneath the earth: And lest thou lift up thine eyes unto heaven, and when thou seest the sun, and the moon, and the stars, even all the host of heaven, shouldest be driven to worship them, and serve them, which the Lord thy God hath divided unto all nations under the whole heaven." Some would venture to say, "It's all Old Testament." Then you should appreciate the gravity of Romans 1:17-25. I feel it exposes the "why" behind God's temptation control with the "images."

It begins reading "**the just shall live by faith**. For the wrath of God is revealed from heaven against all ungodliness and unrighteousness of men, who hold the truth in unrighteousness; Because that which may be known of God is manifest in them; for God hath showed it unto them. For the invisible things of Him from the creation of the world are clearly seen, being understood by the things that are made, even his eternal power and Godhead; so that they are without excuse: Because that, when they knew God, they glorified him not as God, neither were thankful; but became vain in their imaginations, and their foolish heart was darkened. **Professing themselves to be wise, they became fools**, And **changed the glory of the incorruptible God into an image made like** to corruptible man, and to birds, and four-footed beasts, and creeping things. Wherefore God also gave them up to uncleanness through the lusts of their own hearts, to dishonor their own bodies between themselves. **Who changed the truth of God into a lie, and worshipped and served the creature more than the Creator**, who is blessed for ever. Amen."

So, to us, it first sets up that we trust the Word by faith. Second, it explains why we all pick out our particular favorite creation figure: God's attributes are seen throughout all creation! One person is drawn to the peace and serenity of a butterfly. Another sees power and mystique through the bear or the nobility of an elk. Some draw peace when beholding mountains and streams, and some need the simplicity of a meadow as it portrays no burdens, gracefulness, and unobstructed beauty. These qualities, which we each individually see, mean something to us alone. We see things that fill our voids, things that make us sigh with peace or love, things that cause us to feel awe or power, things that solely feed a wild desire for thrill, or things that merely cause a magical or mysterious sense to stir. All these characteristics are not original with us. They all point to God's magnificent wholeness. "For the invisible things of Him from the creation of the world are clearly seen, being understood by the things that are made." None of us would ever dare say we are worshipping or upholding it as more than God. However, too often those chosen "figureheads" don't really remind us *every time* of God. Eventually we are tempting ourselves to draw more and more importance from that creation rather than God Himself. In addition, we cannot honestly judge *ourselves* in this manner of deciding where we are in the spectrum of reverencing a creation object.

God spoke this second commandment to His people. Perhaps it was a commandment to protect those who are weaker, those he knew would struggle with this discretion. But He still chose to command it to ALL His people. We don't see why this is so fought against. If all the stronger aren't tempted this way, we are supposed to help each other out. If our submissive example helps encourage and protect the weaker from an idolatrous practice, then it's worth the inconvenience and attacks of believers and nonbelievers practicing the current traditions. Mostly, if we understand that God's thoughts and ways are so much higher than ours, than how do we begin to take away from His Word? Why not trust it is either for our benefit or another's benefit. And are we not supposed to be working toward another's good? Does not Paul teach in Corinthians to not seek our own "profit, but the profit of many, that they may be saved" (1 Corinthians 10:33)?

3. *"Thou shalt not take the name of the Lord thy God in vain: for the Lord will not hold him guiltless that taketh his name in vain"* (Exodus 20:7). Don't use His name as a curse, don't talk evil of Him. Don't *claim* to have Jesus in your heart and continue disobeying His statutes, because then we become a stumbling block as we misuse His holy name.

4. *"Remember the Sabbath day, to keep it holy. Six days shalt thou labor, and do all thy work: But the seventh day is the Sabbath of the Lord thy God: in it thou shalt not do any work, thou, nor thy son, nor thy daughter, thy manservant, nor thy maidservant, nor thy cattle, nor thy stranger that is within thy gates: For in six days the Lord made heaven and earth,*

the sea, and all that is in them, and rested the seventh day: wherefore the Lord blessed the Sabbath day, and hallowed it" (Exodus 20:8-11). To understand the Sabbath we could look at synonyms for "hallow": make sacred, consecrate, sanctify, bless, make holy...The Lord "set the seventh day apart" from all other six days. This day is different. The scripture says to do no work. So we believe no personal burdensome work should be done that can be done on another day. The seventh day is a privilege to observe as a day set apart to rest as God rested from creation and set this example. Isaiah 58:13-14 encourages us in how to hold a Sabbath: "If thou turn away thy foot on the Sabbath, *from* doing thy pleasure on my holy day; and call the Sabbath a delight, the holy of the Lord, honorable; and shalt honor Him, not doing thine own ways, nor finding thine own pleasure, nor speaking *thine own* words: Then shalt thou delight thyself in the Lord; and I will cause thee to ride upon the high places of the earth, and feed thee with the heritage of Jacob thy father: for the mouth of the Lord hath spoken it." Ezekiel chapter twenty reads, "Moreover, also I gave them my Sabbaths, to be a sign between me and them, that they might know that I am the Lord that sanctifies them" (Ezekiel 20:12).

The Bible says the seventh day is the Sabbath. Our calendar says Saturday is the seventh day of the week. It seems all denominations and various differing religious groups we inquired of all agreed that the seventh day is Saturday, but they chose to hold Sunday, the first day of the week, to celebrate the resurrection of Christ, from scriptures calling for collections on the first day, or showing that some meetings were held on the first day.

We have felt the strength and blessings of observing consistent Sabbaths devoted to God and each other's growth (this blessing comes to those who worship on Saturday or Sunday). Our Sabbath meal is prepared the day(s) before for a quick, effortless meal that we do not have to take time out of the day to make. God gave us this day to draw us closer to Him. He knew we would be busy and needed help to rest and realign our priorities for the next week. This day is not bondage, it is a relief. God's rules help us to become better Christians, He knows best.

I love that God inspired Paul to state in Romans 14:5-6, "One man esteemeth one day above another: another esteemeth every day alike. Let every man be fully persuaded in his own mind. He that regardeth the day, regardeth it unto the Lord; and he that regardeth not the day, to the Lord he doth not regard it. He that eateth, eateth to the Lord, for he giveth God thanks, and he that eateth not, to the Lord he eateth not, and giveth God thanks." Self righteousness leads us to think we have it all figured out so we can tell the hand to be conformed to the foot or they are of no use. Have you not read in 1Corinthians 12:25, where the Holy Spirit has put for you and me to know "that there should be no schism in the body; but that the members should have the same care one for another. And whether one member suffer, all the members suffer with it; or one member be honored, all the members rejoice with it." Shame on Christians to make the body of Christ into divisions. Is Christ divided? (1Corinthians 1:10-19) No, we are all many members of the same body of JESUS CHRIST, so let the hand be a hand unto the Lord, and an eye be an eye unto the Lord.

We need to quit exalting what we see in part over what Christ did in whole.

We believe that the point is to keep the Sabbath and to be steadfast in the day you choose. Colossians 2:16 informs us to not judge another "…in meat, or in drink, or in respect of a holyday, or of the new moon, or of the Sabbath days: Which are a shadow of things to come; but the body is of Christ." We no longer live in bondage but freedom through Christ to each grow in grace, knowledge, and love.

5. *"Honor thy father and thy mother: that thy days may be long upon the land which the Lord thy God giveth thee"* (Exodus 20:12). No matter how old or young you are, if you honor God, you will honor your parents, even if they are not Christians. There is no exception. It does not say, "Honor thy father and mother unless they are not Christians" or "honor thy father and mother unless they are in jail."(1Peter 2:17) They all need cared for, especially when aged (read also Mark 7:9-13). There is a lesson of love here to mould your heart into a heart fit for His kingdom here on earth and in heaven. It honors God when you revere, or respect, His children, whom He created everyone to be. Letting Christ live through you will help you appreciate God's passionate love for your parents and *every* person. Seeing through God's glasses helps us understand each individual for his created potential. It is amazing! We should all ask to have His spiritual eyes.

6. *"Thou shalt not kill"* (Exodus 20:13). There is more to this than just physical death. There can be death to one's spirit and soul as well. Slander, gossip, voicing of opinions, telling

jokes are all examples that could lead to mockery or disbelief in the scriptures, or killing self esteem, which inhibits one to love himself as God does. Jesus teaches us to guard our tongue: "But I say unto you, That every idle word that men shall speak, they shall give account thereof in the day of judgment. For by thy words thou shalt be justified, and by thy words thou shalt be condemned" (Matthew 12:36-37). "Death and life are in the power of the tongue…" (Proverbs 18:21). We must be careful of another's soul and God's reputation as well as created life. We must not destroy any of these.

7. *"Thou shalt not commit adultery"* (Exodus 20:14) Jesus taught us that even a lustful thought is adultery (Matthew 5:28). Marrying a divorced person is adultery (Matthew 5:32). Idolatry is adultery against God.

8. *"Thou shalt not steal"* (Exodus 20:15). Trust God for your provisions and be not covetous for the things God has not given you. Seek first the kingdom of God and what you need to eat, drink, or wear will be added to you (Matthew 6:33) and with these things be content (1 Timothy 7:8).

9. *"Thou shalt not bear false witness against thy neighbor"* (Exodus 20:17). Remember the verse "Death and life are in the power of the tongue: and they that love it shall eat the fruit thereof" (Proverbs 18:21). Being always in God's presence, when we speak negatively or gossip, we are bringing those accusations/judgments before His throne, against our "neighbors." In the measure we judge, we will be judged. Rather, perfect love would turn the other cheek

and be wronged as well as bring out the gold in another person's life. Even in the midst of persecution, love does not notice offenses, and permits the river to flow with forgiveness and patience. This commandment is as much for our own good as our neighbors'.

10. *"Thou shalt not covet thy neighbor's house, thou shalt not covet thy neighbor's wife, nor his manservant, nor his maidservant, nor his ox, nor his ass, nor any thing that is thy neighbor's"* (Exodus 20:17). This commandment is too easily overlooked and not taken seriously. Be content with what God has given you. There may be a good reason you do not have the things your neighbor has. And then, with what God has given you, be ready to gift it away since it's not yours anyway. If we are truly dead to "self" and made alive in God's spirit, then we shouldn't be looking at material worldly things. Surrender your plans and dreams to God and permit God to guide you where He wants your light to shine. For Paul and Peter, that meant they shone in prison for awhile.

1 John 3:23-24 says "this is His commandment, That we should believe on the name of His Son Jesus Christ, and love one another, as He gave us commandment. And he that keepeth His commandments dwelleth in Him and He in him. And hereby we know that He abideth in us, by the Spirit which He hath given us." Jesus said, "Thou shalt love the Lord thy God with all thy heart, and with all thy soul, and with all thy mind. This is the first and great commandment. And the second is like it, Thou shalt love thy neighbor as thyself. On these two commandments hang all the law and the prophets." It's so relieving to be liberated from the *works* of

the law—from the flesh. We are free to live in the spirit, as a new creation under grace, through our Savior Jesus Christ. Galations 2:15—through chapter three—wonderfully explains the transfer from law to faith.

There are promises for those who follow these directives. In the last book in the Bible, Jesus tells His church that He will come quickly "and my reward is with me, to give every man according as his work shall be. I am the Alpha and Omega, the beginning and the end, the first and the last." "Blessed are they that do His commandments, they may have right to the tree of life, and may enter in through the gates into the city." (Revelation 22:12-14) What encouragement to be God's children and to continue following His *house rules*! We are told in the Gospel of John, chapter fifteen, that if "ye keep my commandments, ye shall abide in my love; even as I have kept my Father's commandments, and abide in his love. These things have I spoken unto you, that my joy might remain in you, and that your joy might be full."

What's it all come down to? We should follow the Ten Commandments—and the health message—as wise guidelines, but we should accomplish this because we are focusing our lives on Love—dying to self. Then, we can be confident that we will fulfill all the other commandments God wants us to. It won't be confusing. Correct priorities keep everything in its rightful arrangement. With our single eye focused on God—not a single commandment—we can be filled with His love so we can *walk* in His love, *be* love, and act in faith. The blessings are so rewarding! Our prayer is that our Lord's joy might remain in us, and you.

CHAPTER 10

Accelerated Learning, Part II:
Lessons Learned

While mining, we took it as our responsibility to get the house loan paid down as quickly as possible. First, we promptly tithed from the money Luke brought home. Then, after paying the bills we would make second house payments on the principal only. This stewardship enabled us to pay down nearly $18,000 the first year. We strove to not be materialistic, although Luke did gift me a piano. We had always wanted one, and although we didn't know how to play, we are currently learning.

All our seeking and studying brought along continuous reformation. It did not come all at the same time though, for God will only give us what we can handle (1 Corinthians 10:13). Nevertheless, one blessed correction followed another. We loved that our Holy Teacher was steadily refining us. In fact, during these times when a lull came, we learned to check and make sure we were not drifting our attention off His word to worry ourselves with worldly matters. It's crucial to be attentive for His small voice for He will not yell above the distractions of life.

One of the most recent purchases our Father laid on our hearts to get (in 2008) was *Financial Freedom* by Jim Sammons. It was wonderful! We thought it would talk of money, but it spoke about life principles also. It taught about being lenders, not borrowers, to owe no man anything, how to develop the full potential of your home, family, partnerships, cosigning, tithing, and the list goes on and on. Guess what? If you make a payment and still owe a balance after that payment then you are in debt! Revelation! "No man can serve two masters: for either he will hate the one and love the other; or else he will be loyal to the one, and despise the other. Ye cannot serve God and riches" (Matthew 6:24, Luke 16:13). As soon as we were in debt, we were slaves to money. Thus, our life was not **flexible** for God's direction as He pleases. It's stuck in serving that debt until freed. No, we are not useless to God if we have debt, but we certainly are limited for Him. This lesson is particularly important and unique. We wish our family heritage to know the truth concerning debt and never have to feel the bondage of continuous payments that shift your priorities and feel like a straight jacket.

We only had the house loan, but we felt the burden greatly. It never felt like it was God's best. We couldn't pick up and leave to help someone if we needed to because the debt tied us down. We also learned that by becoming a slave to the world we greatly stole God's glory. We couldn't trust *His* plan, and He *does* have one! We wanted to do something, and instead of waiting and watching God's power, we took the control into our own hands. We went to obtain a loan to buy a house. We had begun to listen to the worldly counsel instead of listening to or seeking biblical counsel. It was, after all, "normal to buy a house in this manner." Normal for who? The world or God? Remember Isaiah 55:8? It says "For my thoughts are not your thoughts, neither are your ways my ways, saith the Lord." We had made a mistake. We sinned by disobeying God's word of instruction. We felt the red flag but ignored it. We clearly saw the folly in debt. Repentant, we purposed to sell the house and never go into debt again. A scripture comes to mind often that reminds us of our quest: "For the eyes of the Lord run to and fro throughout the whole earth, to show Himself strong in the behalf of them whose heart is perfect toward Him…" (2 Chronicles 16:9). We want to be dependent upon God's power, free from debt and a full time job, to go immediately where God needs us. We want to be the children that He sees as He "looks to and fro."

At first, mining life seemed to go fine except the odd, alternating shift hours. This caused great inconsistencies and only allowed a few hours of time with the family a day. All the same, God was answering our prayers and teaching us what it meant to be a biblical family. My turn to conform to God's standard of biblical womanhood and virtuous wife was first. Let's explain it this way. Our hearts can be a place of grand exquisite landscaping…*if*…if we allow Jesus to come in and clean us out and God to mercifully design and artistically sculpt us.

When we allow our Great Gardener in, the first thing that needs to happen is preparing the soil. To do this, old weeds need to be pulled. These weeds are our worldly ways, ideas, pleasures, identities, and idols. At first we are excited and even help pull up and throw away weeds, but when just a corner of the easiest are pulled, we come to a few deeply rooted plants. They hurt to be pulled, because they're our past history, our habits, old traditions, and former way of life. We tend to panic, as without these plants it leaves us in the unknown; it leaves us with no control and no self identity. In a panic we wrestle with the Gardner and grab onto the roots to secure them. After all, our *fear* says that plant is okay. But wait! God says it must be replaced, and we must trust Him. *Fear* causes us to explain to *God* that *He* must be mistaken as those particular plants are indigenous, and *He* doesn't understand our situation and how *our* plans need it, or how it doesn't need pulled because it's been there so long, and it's not hurting anything. Fear is *not* from God. However, our patient Father will not force us to do anything. He may wonder where all our trust and zeal went, though.

Our soul is God's garden. Sometimes people use it as a dump and pollute it with evil materials. Sometimes we attempt to landscape it. Sometimes we are lazy and neglect it. Sometimes we just cover it up in an effort to live peacefully and with the least confrontations possible. But don't be fooled, it *will* be landscaped. The question is **who is your Gardener?** All the self-searching, self-help books, or really, *any* resources outside the Bible, are unable to create the prize unless you crave a garden of fire and brimstone. All our knowledge and transplanting and replacing are to no avail. We are unable to learn how the soul needs tended. That is, until we ask God. God created the soul. Only He knows how to garden it so everything works toward good. Only He knows the final purpose for each of us. He will teach us how to watch for noxious weeds that hurt our soul. Our faithful Father is ready to tend all of our gardens. We just need to step aside and trust the Master's hands... And, He will only give us what we can bear. The *Holy Word* says that we have no uncommon temptation and God, who is faithful, will provide a way to escape that temptation (1 Corinthians 10:13).

In my life, when those deep roots were pulled, it stirred up the ground around it. I remember this discomfort and turmoil as distrust in my Father in Heaven. He was showing me His beautiful creation, not as I would see it, but as He intended it to be. My Father did not start at this time alone. He had begun my training years ago, but I was now in training full time.

It is very interesting how women *want* to manage and have their say-so in everything that their husbands, their family, and they themselves do. I've been there. We "meekly" push from behind, nag by repeating our opinions several times, we argue, we even belittle. Some pretend they are more spiritual. Some have mini fits. Some cry unfairness. We are all sinners, and we are all *wrong*—not wrong to be communicating, but wrong in the manner we do it. We all want a supreme position in our husbands' hearts. What most don't realize is under the self-attempts to *make* our marriages heavenly, we are the very cause of the lack of "oneness."

I purposed to be a wife after God's own heart and relinquish authority and vision to my husband. Our Father in Heaven doesn't tell me to be submissive and honor our husbands only when he is doing what I would. It's all the time, "in everything" (Ephesians 5:22-24). Through better and worse I am to respect his authority and honor his position and headship given to *him*, not me (as long as he is not violating God's scriptures).

If you have just begun to allow your husband to hold the reigns, realize the vulnerable position he is in and guard yourself. Your old nature wants to critically watch his every move so your heart can say "I told you so." Yes, verbally spoken or not, your heart has sinned if this happens. Biting your tongue is not the joyful, content, submissive, and meek wife God wants for your husband. Who can perform at his best when someone standing so close is waiting for him to mess up, then to snatch the reigns back the moment pressure causes a stumble?

A wonderful thing occurs when we turn our hearts to God—a beautiful transformation. When we are content, when we enjoy our husbands and thank our husbands and adore our husbands for the position they have *over* us, we are truly turning our hearts to God. We are focusing our eyes to correct ourselves and not to sculpt our husbands (which oftentimes suffocates them and renders them helpless for God's use). When I worked on the plank in my own eye (Matthew 7:5) and allowed my Father to conform my heart, my beloved husband gave me "queen-ship." He will now confide in me, and he will seek out my advice constantly. I no longer feel it necessary to give advice, but am free to smile into his loving face and even tell him I'll follow whichever decision he chooses. This trusting in Him which God has given me puts an adorable shine in his eyes, and I wonder why it took me so long to find joy in being under my husband's authority. My trust in him enables him to bring me alongside to be *one* with him.

Each time, I am in awe of God's reforming my "garden." How much better it is! How I rejoice to see God's masterful plan unfold as my seeking to gain wisdom is granted, and His mercy uncovers and lays out one more little section of "garden." I learn quickly the breathtaking beauty of God's design. It is so exquisite, so peaceful, so happy, such a blessing. I yearn to learn more just to allow God to re-create my former drab soul into His work of art. I say it is beautiful, not because I think I'm special or "arrived," but because I know my life is lining up with God's instruction more and more. Our souls crave fulfillment in finding and living in the purpose that God has created for each of us: a role specific for females and a role specific for males. And they beautifully complement each other in a true *oneness* marriage. It's not any different for those who are single. God is then your spouse from whom you get that intimate oneness from. Even for men, it is available.

My "garden," my soul, still has much that needs conformed, and all of it needs constant tending or bad weeds will sneak their way in. In fact, when a trial comes, Luke and I together try to remember to praise God because He is stepping in to help us tend our garden and pull our "noxious weeds." The Word says "For whom the Lord loves he disciplines, and scourges every son whom He receives" (Hebrews 12:6), and, "For whom the Lord loves he corrects; even as a father his son in whom he delighteth" (Proverbs 3:12). What an absolute wonderful sense to know God loves us. Thank you, Father, for teaching us! Thank you for loving us! Thank you for saying "no" to us! Thank you, Father, forever!

We share the hardships we have had to encourage you and because we get to share the beauty of togetherness and the beauty of God's design. Even though we *still* continually strive for that oneness, as marriage must always be worked at, today I am breathless at the heavenly marriage we get to experience. God is helping us to melt together, to communicate.

One more note: it is true that a wife is not a cookie cutter. She must be the helper *her* husband needs. Many women have tried to copy another in hopes it would help their marriage or to keep up with the Jones'. Men require different things. Mine likes to be in the kitchen and help with *all* household duties if not otherwise busy. He even prefers to make breakfast for the whole family, while another wants his wife to perform all the chef/home duties. So my spare time is neither to be coveted nor despised as laziness. Nor should I covet another woman, whose husband seems to need her more than mine. These are Satan's lies to cause discontentment in us. My point is that each wife is given to her husband to fulfill *his* personal needs, wants, and visions. Women should not compare themselves with other women; they should compare their hearts with scripture. Sometimes I ask myself, "If Luke died right now, could I say I was God's best for him?" What regrets, issues, thoughts, or praises come to mind at that question? Then I can deal with them and become, or maintain, being God's best for him.

As I have learned the glory of being Luke's helpmeet, he has learned the newfound duty of leadership. This patriarchal vision is as lost to the world as a submissive wife. Men are only too quick to be quiet/passive, and complacent. They may not even realize their lack of involvement. It takes true reformation for a *man* to turn his heart toward his family. It's true there are males in this society, but true *men* are hard to find. Men who live the Bible, men who stand up and put on the armor of God as it says in Ephesians 6:11, "Put on the whole armor of God, that ye may be able to stand against the wiles of the devil." "Stand therefore, having girded your waist with truth, and having on the breastplate of righteousness; and your feet shod with the preparation of the gospel of peace; above all, taking the shield of faith, wherewith ye shall be able to quench all the fiery darts of the wicked. And take the helmet of salvation, and the sword of the Spirit, which is the Word of God: Praying always with all prayer...watching with all perseverance..." (Ephesians 6:14-18). God needs men, who demonstrate godly manliness as they put women and children before their own lives. He needs men who are ready to lay down their lives to live for God through His scriptures, to nurture and admonish their children, to exhort and join with their wives. God needs men to live the life of Christ as leaders and servants, just as real godly women should live the life of Christ through humble submissiveness and obedience.

My sons and daughters have a real man as a father who shows my sons godly manhood and sets a standard to the minimum type of husband our daughters will accept. No, he is not perfect. Sometimes he has been quite the "bull-in-a-china-cabinet" where my heart is concerned. He *is* human. However, I would choose to marry him even more now than ever before. I am so thankful that Luke recognized our weapon of warfare: prayer. Luke rightfully takes my hand and together we go to God as our strength and our help. This way, when no other answers arrive, God remains the mortar of our marriage.

So, husbands, we implore you to always unite yourselves with your wife in prayer. Take her hand in yours and always take everything to God. In this way you can be a formidable force *for* God and *against* Satan, who will assuredly continue to try and break families apart. If he can get the fathers away from the family, to get the children away from the parents, to get wives out from under their authority, if he can dilute, pollute, and destroy the Christian home-centered family, then he will. It's vitally important that fathers step up and "be men" concerning the doctrine. "Brethren, be not children in understanding: howbeit in malice be ye children, but in *understanding* be men" (1Corinthians 14:20). You also have a flock of little sheep who want to give their hearts to you if you will take them, discuss and teach them, *talk* with them, play with them, love them as the Bible says. These are all things Luke has learned and embraced. These revelations and commitments have been building and finally blossomed in August of 2008, where they took firm root. He has been our father and husband and spiritual counselor for years, and his heart was always to have a family business where he could include his children. But life changed and added precept upon precept in 2008.

Of course you know of the ongoing MRSA. It had briefly lessened its attacks to where Luke could continue mining during all new outbreaks and be fine. However, around the end of July, they began to worsen. Luke had a week of vacation coming the beginning of August and hung in until then. For health reasons and not wishing to lower his immunities further and also because we wanted to prove to others that God could heal it on His own or with herbs, we weren't going to use antibiotics. Well, God always knows best.

At the end of the vacation, Luke's MRSA flared up and again was painfully swollen resulting in calling in for "no-pay" days. As company policy required him to see a doctor if two days were missed, Luke went in and was sent home with antibiotics. About this same time Luke was entertaining the possibility of quitting mining. He asked that if he were to quit, God would grant him complete disdain for working underground. We then submitted *our* plans concerning Luke's health and medicine and began taking the antibiotics. We did so with mixed feelings and joked about the irony that since we wanted to show God's power in proving herbs, God would show us *His* power and heal Luke the opposite way we wanted.

As the swelling began to lessen, Luke began to dread his work. He became unhappy, but felt he *had* to go. At a reminder of his fleece to God, he realized the complete revulsion he had for underground mining. He decided to return to work for two more weeks. He put in his notice, but after two days back he inquired at the office and learned he would only have to finish the week. The two week notice was unnecessary. September 2, 2008 marked the day Luke was done mining. He came home to the family. What about his MRSA you ask? It quickly healed up and to date has *never* returned. We learned God does not need *us* to show His power, He can do that on His own, and whether it's herbs, hospital, or miracle, *ALL* healing is to God's credit.

CHAPTER 11

Being about God's Business

I n April 2008 God brought a homeopathic remedy before me. I compared and researched its ingredients. As I learned what each herb had to offer, I became excited about modifying it and making a salve for our family. So, I removed several ingredients from the list and carefully selected my own herbs to compound an efficient salve that would meet several of our family's needs.

One day my mother was describing her friend's ankle pain. I offered some of our salve to see if it would help. Long story short, her friend used it liberally and noticed results within hours! I was well surprised. My mother then sprained her own ankle, and after a few days of pain decided she would try it too (since it worked for her friend). Later she reported to me that "that afternoon I suddenly realized I was walking pain free!" With diligent applications, God healed their infirmities.

I, of course, was sharing these stories with Luke's mom, and she wanted to try it on her strained knee injury that had persisted for months. It took several weeks of usage to show results, but in the end, it was the vessel of healing for her knee. She began sharing her salve with many others and a demand was soon created. Thanks to Mom, the salve was known to others as "Roxy's Miracle Salve." Mom encouraged us to sell our "Roxy's Miracle Salve." We were unsure how to do it, but I realized God had given us the product, tested it, marketed it, set the price for it and was giving us customers before we had the inventory ready. We couldn't believe it. What an answer to prayer! So, with praise to our God, I started production. By word of mouth, we are stewarding God's family business and offering herbal products for the glory of God to others.

We were very excited and thankful for what God was doing. Even though Luke didn't take much part in the business—as he thought it was mine, he still helped me find scriptures to adorn our simple labels. We wanted to give glory to God for the product he had given us. We also dedicated our business to Him and committed to steward it as long as He wanted us to. To remind us of our ethical value and representation of the business, we headed it up with Proverbs 22:1, "A good name is rather to be chosen than great riches." Mom found the packaging for my salves, and through her contribution of our first tins and jars I made some "Roxy's Miracle Salve," filled containers, labeled them and put shrink bands on to finish. Very soon we sold out and had back orders. Realizing the quantity of sales, in July 2008 I finally became a licensed business under the name "Simple Living."

God granted the inspiration of new products for our family. Upon hiking in June, I noticed the need for a safe, natural, and chemical-free bug repellent. And, of course, an organic remedy for insect bites and itching/pain relief was needed, too. "Roxy's Miracle Salve" would work for this too, but I wanted this product to specialize for its purpose in a handy one ounce tin. Following this we made lip balm. And the most recent product is the deodorant, free from aluminum, that we use at home. All these are offered to the public. Other products our family uses, but are not marketing, are homemade toothpaste and homemade laundry soap (see Appendix IV for these fun hand-me-down recipes).

I really wanted to have our children work with me so they felt needed and included. Therefore I made the effort to name some of our products after them to further enable ownership in our business. For example, when our son Malachi was four years old, he liked the idea that God is our King of Kings and that he is His child, thus making him a Prince. So we named the Bite Aid "Princely Bite Aid." When Courage was two years old, he did not like bugs, thus the product "Li'l Courage Bug Repellent." Our five-year-old daughter, Nyomi, is a merry maiden, feminine, and servant-like. We honored her by giving her the flavored "Maiden Lip Balm." However, as men would not enjoy using a woman's balm, we sympathetically made an unflavored "Chap Lip Balm" as a counterpart, as Chap means gentleman. The name "Roxy's Miracle Salve" was originally how my salve was referred, so I kept the title already being used.

We sell colloidal silver water with the slogan "Prudence in every matter" for the double meaning, as Prudence is our second daughter's name. Next, we have "Josiah's Natural Deodorant," Luke's product. Finally, "Titus" is our homemade soap line for our newest baby. Again, this business would not be what it is except for God laying it on Mom's gracious heart to encourage us. She was also our most loyal customer for quite some time! ☺ Thank you, Mom!

One other item God helped me to achieve is a long insulated dress coat trimmed with fake fur. I was inspired to design and custom sew one for Nyomi and myself. We needed to be able to function in cold weather in our dresses and couldn't find what we were looking for. So, with a list of purposes to accomplish, I designed a coat and God blessed the work of my hands as I assembled them. I had a great time! Not being a seamstress, I was not certain how to sew it, but God gave me little instructions for one step at a time. When each step was accomplished, my mind would become blank, and I would know my sewing was complete for the day. Then I would awake the next day with new wisdom of how to continue. Thus God helped me finish our coats. God will always give us the abilities to accomplish the tasks he sets before us! Moreover, my coat of function became fashionable to the inhabitants of the Silver Valley. God brought to me some wonderful customers desiring a quality dress coat for themselves. This helped much toward our finances.

When Luke resigned from his high paying job of mining and came home, he still left the business to me. As we stepped out to live on faith, God began to show more of His power. Working outside the home is not an enemy in itself, but for us, we feel called toward the lifestyle change. It was difficult for Luke because he held his identity and self worth in an occupation rather than God and the family. He, like any other man, wants to provide well for his family. So, the transition from a job to complete trust in God created some trials for him. He would search for a home business to start but worried he didn't have any skills. As each bill came and we paid from our savings, he would panic and want to return to mining, but his convictions and vision would hang before him and prevent further action. During these times God would help me share some strength of faith with my husband to persevere and put our dependence on God. We needed to trust the vision our God has given us.

It always seemed that when we needed encouragement and wondered if we really *were* doing what God asked of us, a miracle would arrive. Our faith was tested and confirmed. Losing the house greatly concerned us, but we had to obey the promptings of our Lord. Yes, we had to let God be more important than our home and pride. Every bill brought us to our knees for communion with God as we weren't sure how the next one was going to be paid. About a month after Luke received his final paycheck, we received another check from the US Silver Mines for $250. Out of the blue, God provided $250! What a miracle! It was such wonderful encouragement. God was confirming our direction. Luke really needed it, too; as it was particularly hard to be humbly steadfast while outsiders thought he was irresponsible. Just the weight of that "stare" he received so often nearly made him return to the mines so he could feel "normal."

Following closely to this miracle was another. As I was beginning to pay our bills one day, I started with telephone banking to double check the activity in our account. When I finished there was $250 extra. We couldn't believe it. We decided to sit on it in case an error had occurred, but a few days later I was again on the phone with the bank. I had already checked my records back one full year and I had everything the bank did and all was accounted for. Talking with customer service, we went over our account and she kept saying it *was* our true balance and possibly my math needed checked. Praise the Lord! We are so humbled at the hand of God. We are so far from perfect and yet our Father is always with us. Out of nothing, God provided us another $250.

Just as the Israelites saw God part the sea before them and thereafter did not trust, saw manna fall from heaven, water come from a rock, and their clothes never wore out, they still always grumbled. They never remembered, they forgot to have faith. Just like the Israelites, after we paid our bills we would forget what He had done and think God couldn't handle our next bill. We had to submit our fears again and trust God. First Timothy 6:8 says "And having food and clothing let us therewith be content." God has promised to provide His children with food and clothing, as Jesus taught in Luke 12:22-31: "...take no thought for your life, what ye shall eat; neither for the body, what ye shall put on. The life is more than food and the body is more than raiment. Consider the ravens: for they neither sow nor reap; which neither have storehouse nor barn; and God feedeth them: how much more are ye better than the fowls? And which of you with taking thought can add to his stature one cubit? If ye then be not able to do that thing which is the least, why take ye thought for the rest? Consider the lilies how they grow: they toil not, they spin not; and yet I say unto you, that Solomon in all his glory was not arrayed like one of these. If then God so clothes the grass, which is today in the field, and tomorrow is cast into the oven; how much more will he clothe you, O ye of little faith? And seek not ye what ye shall eat, or what ye shall drink, neither be ye of a doubtful mind. For all these things the nations of the world seek after: and your Father knoweth that you have need of these things. But rather seek ye the kingdom of God; and all these things shall be added unto you."

We shop for the needs of our house one time each month. This includes everything from soap and toilet paper to grocery items. With faith, we believe God's promise and do not worry about keeping a budget for food and clothing, but instead ask God to provide what we need or stretch our money as we go shopping. Again, the power of God is more than *we* can understand. Even though we had five eating members in our family at this time, we went from spending $350-$400 a month to spending $70 for everything we needed for the whole month. God blessed our storehouse as neighbors occasionally brought over food items and our buckets of grains and oats seemed to never deplete. Three months in a row we spent $70. In one of those months we happened to be getting a dryer, and the sellers had apple trees. They asked us to take as many apples as we could. We came home that day rich in fruit and the blessings of God. We had *just* run out of applesauce and fruit, and God replenished our supply through those apples.

A wonderful new epiphany took root in our lives: God is in control of everything. We knew this before, but again God proved it to us and it took deeper root. What a love our Father has for His children! The money we needed to pay our bills consistently came in one week before they were due, enabling us to never pay late. When Luke first quit working, we were desperate and felt lost in a maze of dark tunnels. But because of our assurance that God was with us, we quickly learned to *cling* to our Guide.

At the end of October, Luke decided he needed to spend several days in the mountain with God for personal searching and prayer. Hence, with his Bible and blankets, he headed off. Upon his return he finally felt peace about his decisions. (You can find his notes concerning this time in Appendix II.) He resolved to not get a forty-hour-per-week job *unless* we could no longer pay our bills. With that settled, he could relax and be content to unite the family under God and thank God for his current time with us.

Although we still can't figure *exactly* how it happened, God continued providing exactly what we needed. Those times were so joyous. Sure, we had to really watch all our activities and eat a little differently, but we finished our meals full every day, and we were living our dream of working and remaining as a family. All our hearts were knit together, and that is more than worth it.

This humble business is completely God's. He works through it for us. Business grows when we need it to, and it stays quiet when God supplies Luke with other income endeavors. If we are supplied with extra cash, we try to prayerfully hold and consider how God would want us to steward it. Sometimes it's for our bills, and He wants to see us care for it as such. Sometimes God may provide extra because He has plans for us to help another child of His. Sometimes it is for our wants: here's an event I clearly see God's hand in.

I really wanted to go to Luke's mom's house because it had been *quite* some time since we had visited her. Since we had to go to Spokane for groceries, we would be halfway to her home. Luke vetoed the idea, as he didn't like the extra gas expense. While in Spokane, we stayed a night at Dad (Luke's dad) and Caron's house as planned. The next day a snowstorm hit earlier than expected. We rushed through our grocery shopping, but the few hours it took were enough for the roads in Spokane and the I-90 Freeway to begin shutting down. We *had* to go to Luke's moms! I don't think the snowstorm was just for me, but I do see God's handiwork in orchestrating the events. We got to spend three days with Mom, enjoying helping her shovel and being "snowed-in" there, before it was safe to return. It was a great stay!

Just after this, during the 2009 New Year, Luke's brother's and sister's families were gathering at Moms. We really wanted to visit and see them all, but had *zero* funds for gas. We asked God to provide the gas money if He wanted us to go. If not, it was completely okay. That very night before the gathering came a few sales. It was not enough to satisfy Luke, so we figured it wasn't a green light to go. The next day around mid-morning came in another sale, and Luke decided we would make the trip. It turned out gas was cheaper on the way home, and we had extra money when the trip was over!

So, we have learned to prayerfully consider and ask God of our plans before carrying them out. We can trust Him. With our four children, ages one to six years, we are experiencing the beauty of togetherness, the blessings of our olive plants (Psalm 127). We are experiencing the splendor of having the hearts of our children knit *together* and *all of our* hearts intertwined as a real family.

CHAPTER 12

Victory over Darkness

As you learn new concepts in the Bible, as God unlocks new convictions of His word and love, as you attempt to follow God and become "hot" instead of "luke-warm," you can also be sure Satan will be trying to make you fall. He promised in Revelation 12:17 that he would "…make war with the remnant of her seed, which keep the commandments of God, and have the testimony of Jesus Christ." When you become steadfast for God's Holy Word, Satan panics because he is losing another battle. Satan will attack you and try to pull you away. He will try by creating pride. He'll try by creating a bad self image with depression or guilt. He'll try by causing you to forget your value and worth in God's eyes, to forget God's love for you. Satan will try to stop your actions of righteous faith by giving confusion, busyness, rationalizations, and compromised excuses.

God's ways *may* bring persecution and inconvenience since you are peculiar to the world, but your peculiarity (for obeying the commandments) is a *beautiful* thing to the Lord and is a sign to Him of your heart towards Him. If you are about God's business, then you should "let your light so shine before men, that they may see your good works, and glorify your Father which is in Heaven" (Matthew 5:16).

What's our life purpose? To glorify God and do *His good* deeds. What should be the result of our actions? It should be praise and glory to our "Father which is in Heaven." How do we know God's Will? Seek after Him and read His Word, the Bible. God's light will shine, and love will be spread, but if you walk another path, the path where Satan has befuddled *your* reasons, *your* agenda, *your* life, because you are fighting for your *earthly* things (including your life), then contentions and strife follow in your associations with men. But in *your* righteousness, it's hard to see the problem.

As scales cover your eyes, you no longer remember to "let it go." "I say unto you, that ye resist not evil: but whosoever shall smite thee on thy right cheek, turn to him the other also. And if any man will sue thee at the law, and take away thy coat, let him thy cloak also. If any man shall compel thee to go a mile, go with him two" (Matthew 5:39-41). Seek God, let the scales fall. See God's bigger picture. "Blessed are the peacemakers: for they shall be called the children of God" (Matthew 5:9). "...I say unto you, Love your enemies, bless them that curse you, show good to them that hate you, and pray for them which despitefully use you, and persecute you; that you may be the children of your Father which is in heaven..." (Mathew 5:44-45) Why? So you can be counted His children.

What did Jesus do when the Jews killed Him? He loved them and prayed for them. This is the standard *we* need to keep. This is the light we need to show before men that they may glorify our Father which is in Heaven. This is the ultimate love challenge. Thus, "agree with your adversary quickly, while thou art in the way with him; lest at any time the adversary deliver thee to the judge, and the judge deliver thee to the officer, and thou be cast into prison. Verily I say unto thee, Thou shalt by no means come out thence, until thou hast paid the utmost farthing" (Matthew 5: 25-26). Although we know the pleasures and blessings of being God's children, these enjoyments exist because Christ gave His life for us. Remember, humility must be continually practiced and is never *really* mastered.

God warned that we shouldn't argue or continue with strife "for we wrestle not against flesh and blood, but against principalities, against powers, against the rulers of the darkness of this world, against spiritual wickedness..." (Ephesians 6:12). Complaining, replaying past hurts, or speaking negatively means you are entertaining the devil at your table. God, our Father, told his children to speak differently from the world. "When you come together, each one has a hymn, a lesson, a revelation, a tongue, or an interpretation. Let all things be done for building up" (1 Corinthians 14:26). "Let no corrupting talk come out of your mouths, but only such as is good for building up, as fits the occasion, that it may give grace to those who hear" (Ephesians 4:29). "So then let us pursue what makes for peace and for mutual up-building" (Romans 14:19). "Finally, brothers, whatever is true, whatever is honorable, whatever is just, whatever is pure, whatever is lovely, whatever is commendable, if there is any excellence, if there is anything worthy of praise, think about these things" (Philippians 4:8).

Here's the key to controlling your thoughts so you can speak from a pure heart and not let there be a door for Satan to open into your life: words. They are the fruit of the spirits you entertain. Principalities, remember? You must know your Father, through Jesus, to stand in your rightful identity as a worthy son and daughter—to combat the enemy. Let the Word be your strong fortress and let the Word abide in you. This will help your words be the "sword of truth" against evil.

Furthermore, God says his children know His voice and follow it. It is more than coincidence that the preceding scripture is the preparation for war: "Put on the whole armor of God that ye may be able to stand against the wiles of the devil" (Ephesians 6:11). And Ephesians 6:14 begins the instruction of how to arm yourself against these spiritual wars: "Stand therefore, having girded your waist with truth, and having on the breastplate of righteousness; and your feet shod with the preparation of the gospel of peace; above all, taking the shield of faith, wherewith ye shall be able to quench all the fiery darts of the wicked. And take the helmet of salvation, and the sword of the Spirit, which is the Word of God: Praying always with all prayer…watching with all perseverance…" (Ephesians 6:14-18). Pride pulls us away from God and causes us to make the wrong stands concerning our dealings with men. Be the best slave of the *Holy Word,* and experience the freedom!

During July to August 2008, I personally experienced the helplessness of *myself* and the *power* of Christ's Redeeming blood. This "time" overlapped the climax of the preceding chapter where our several trials were unfolding themselves into new refined understandings. I have only shared this once before, and am sharing it to you so you can know there *are* principalities at war for your soul.

This particular day Luke was working afternoon swing shift, leaving at 3pm and coming home around 4am in the morning. After he left, the day continued as normal, but with an atmosphere of "aloneness." This didn't hinder the kids and me from enjoying our family fun. Eight o'clock soon came around, and our wonderful children were happily tucked in bed and quickly fast asleep.

Immediately my loneliness turned to an unsettled feeling. I made the rounds to make sure all the doors and windows were locked, as I was certain a robber was lurking outside. I knew fear is not from God, so I confessed this temptation to my Father in Heaven, my Protector, and decided to go downstairs to sew as planned. The unsettled feeling continued and I desperately wanted to call some friends who could pray and help me spiritually, as I suspected this *was* a spiritual matter. However, I felt embarrassed and thought no one would understand, or would think I was weird. I thought I was weak for not handling this on my own, for not having enough faith to believe God was enough. The need to contact someone became more urgent as the talons of fear gripped me. I abandoned my sewing, as I wasn't getting much done anyway, to go upstairs and be closer to my children. I wanted to call Luke at work but knew he was out of reach.

As I came upstairs, I saw my Bible and was prompted to get it. I sensed there would be comfort there, but as I closed the door I again thought how weak I was because I couldn't have the faith for God to protect me. When the door closed I began to feel surrounded, and panic was nearly overwhelming. Glancing from the Bible I went to my bedroom to retrieve a pistol for protection. As I calmly took hold of my gun, I was prompted to put it away.

I was convinced somebody was going to break-in any moment. I remember the suffocation I was feeling, the evil surroundings of desperation wanting to crowd me. The air seemed incredibly *heavy* and thick, and there seemed to be a great weight around me. Even though I had every single light in the house *on*, I can remember the dimness like the last rays fading at dusk. Although fear *wanted* to captivate me, I could also feel wrapped in the close communion of God. This was my lifeline. I stood there with my hand on the gun when the understanding came that the protection I needed would not come from the gun, and suddenly I felt that the urge to carry it was from Satan. I put it away and stood there for a few seconds… The Holy Ghost told me the house needed to be cleansed of evil. I knew the blood of Jesus was my power and salvation, that His blood overcomes evil.

I was prompted, "Go get the Bible, it will give you strength."

I understood the Holy Spirit wanted me to take the Bible to each room and cleanse it with the blood of Jesus, "but how?"

"Get something to anoint the room."

"But what?" I hesitated.

"Perfume, body spray, anything." I knew I needed to show action.

"But it's not holy water," I thought.

"By the Blood of the Lamb only do you have the power to overcome evil."

I went to retrieve some body spray, but suddenly felt all the hairs on my neck stand on end. I detoured and went straight for my Bible while the claustrophobic feeling actually made it difficult to draw a full breath. The closer I got the more enclosed I became, but I was constantly aware that unless I *gave-in* to fear, nothing would happen as I was being "held up."

The very second I touched my Bible, the air cleared. Dimness turned bright as a clear midday sun. The suffocating, hot, heavy weight upon me instantaneously cleared to abundant space, clean air, and no unsettled fear. I exceedingly thanked God for His Son and worshipped Jesus for His death on the cross and passing the anointing power He received on to us.

I was reminded to proceed. I obtained some spray and wondered where to begin. I wanted to protect the kids but didn't want to wake them. God said, "Go to Nyomi's room, then the boys'." I at once obeyed. In Nyomi's room, with the Holy Spirit and by the blood of Jesus, I urgently proclaimed salvation and came against all evil. Some time was spent in prayer and worship when a peace of freedom was felt, and I "anointed" the room with spray. I then closed the door to a spiritually peaceful and safe room. I continued to the boys' room and prayed, praised, and claimed the power of Jesus' blood against evil therein. After anointing that room, I left it in the most capable hands of our God. I repeated these steps until all 2,068 square feet of home and our surrounding property was evicted of evil and protected by the saving blood of Christ. Where before, I was scared to shut off lights, I now had confidence and assurance and not only went to bed, but slept soundly.

This occurrence is not an event that you should be afraid of. I wish it to prepare your soul to "put on the whole armor of God" (Ephesians 6:11) and combat evil. Have faith and confidence, not in yourself and *your* knowledge, but in saving grace. I am *nobody* in respect of persons. I am a sinner who desperately needs saving grace and forgiveness, but Jesus Christ obediently died on the cross as atonement for my sins too. He overcame death, thus He overcame evil. He offers this atonement and gift of salvation to all, that by His death we are made new creations and righteous before God. "Behold, I stand at the door, and knock: if any man hear my voice, and open the door, I will come in to him, and will [dine] with him, and he with me" (Revelation 3:20). We should all *crave* this Presence and intimate relationship with our Eternal Father. God helped me to be spiritually aware of my surroundings. I purposed to not run during this oppression, as panic attacks are not of God. I had Jesus in my heart and a Rock under my feet. What could happen to me if I trusted my Lord?

I want you to understand that serving Christ is not a mere theory and way of life, it is *real*. The Bible is the only Book where forty different authors from different time spans wrote about the same God, the same Son, the same love, the same judgments, the same end, the same choice: life or death. All you have to do is have faith, and believe what *God's* inspired word says.

What took place that night was *real*. What protects our house is *real*. It wasn't my glory who stood against evil principalities. But it *was* my small faith and obedience that *allowed* Christ's blood, allowed heavenly principalities, to engage in war and drive out evil from our home and keep it as our safe house. The spray and the Bible were *tools* of faith. The spray I used was not in itself significant or necessary. God knew I needed a physical crutch. The perfume itself did nothing as far as driving out evil, *but* the scent of perfume permeating the room symbolized to *me* the finalized fulfilling victory of Good over Evil. Just as the scent of oil filled the air, I know Christ's blood covered and cleansed our home and property. Similarly, the Bible itself cannot combat evil. A book has no power. But to me, the *truth* in the Book reminded me of the saving power of Jesus Christ and His broken body and shed blood. To touch these truths reminded me of the power I had through my salvation, "the only begotten son:" "For God so loved the world, that He gave His only begotten Son, that whosoever believeth in Him should not perish, but have everlasting life. For God sent not his Son into the world to condemn the world; but that the world through Him might be saved" (John 3:16-17).

Men and women, have faith—not in yourselves, but in God who has the power to save you.

"Thou art my God, and I will praise thee: thou art my God, I will exalt thee. O give thanks unto the Lord; for He is good: for His mercy endureth for ever." Psalm 118:28-29

CHAPTER 13

Concerning Tithe and Provisions

I t is amazing to watch God's power, and a merciful blessing to be part of it...

A while ago, we had purchased a generator that makes colloidal silver water which heals several varying ailments. A store we supply with our salves sells colloidal silver items, and although she sold the water as well, it wasn't normally a hot item. One day, we received a phone call and learned the regular supplier of this colloidal silver water backed out. The proposal to us was to become her supplier until her own generator was delivered. She would pay sixteen dollars per sixteen ounces of water. She didn't figure she needed much, "four would be plenty" as it wasn't in high demand. With praises to God, we supplied the water which costs us mere cents per thirty-two ounces to make! We weren't expecting any orders for more, but one week later the owner called to report in amazement that all four sold and she needed four more. Could she pick them up tomorrow? Our eyes were wide open with excitement at this blessing and we chattered to each other of our glorious God.

Three days later she calls again. In shock she laughs as she tells us she doesn't know what is going on, but she *again* sold out and needs more. Her generator hadn't arrived as the company was having computer problems. In thirteen days, God arranged for us to supply a total of eighteen sixteen-ounce bottles of water before her generator was delivered. That's $288. What heavenly provisions!

Early spring of 2009, we received a letter from the IRS. They had audited our 2007 Federal Income Tax Return. The letter said we owed $2,000, besides interest. What a surprise! Before anything else, we took the matter to our God. Then, as I do our taxes myself, I pulled up our records and found an error. I had not recorded the $4,300 we withdrew to close out a Roth IRA investment account, but I had sent in the form with my tax return. I called Waddell and Reed and requested my contribution history. Once received, I amended my taxes to show the correct amount owed. We owed $450, plus interest.

Everything is given to us for a reason so Luke and I discussed why this happened. Was it a test of faith? Were we violating a biblical principle? Were our hearts wrong in tithing—were we not *cheerful* givers, expecting nothing in return? After we prayed about it, we both began checking our tithe history. Had we stolen from God? Malachi 3:7-12 speaks concerning tithe: "Even from the days of your fathers ye are gone away from mine ordinances, and have not kept them. Return unto me, and I will return unto you, saith the Lord of hosts...Will a man rob God? Yet ye have robbed me. But ye say, Wherein have we robbed thee? In tithes and offerings. Ye are cursed with a curse: for ye have robbed me, even this whole nation. Bring ye all the tithes into the storehouse, that there may be meat in mine house, and prove me now herewith, saith the Lord of hosts, if I will not open you the windows of heaven, and pour you out a blessing, that there shall not be room enough to receive it. And I will rebuke the devourer for your sakes, and he shall not destroy the fruits of your ground; neither shall your vine cast her fruit before the time in the field, saith the Lord of hosts. And all the nations shall call you blessed: for ye shall be a delightsome land, saith the Lord of hosts."

We were told a story about a family who had one abnormal expense after another. He complained of this to his Christian neighbor. The neighbor asked his friend if he was tithing. The friend responded with "I can't afford to tithe!" He had vehicle repairs, doctor bills, house repairs, etc., etc. The neighbor explained the important principle of tithing. He then proposed an experiment and his friend consented. That night the family put together all their current income and their unusual costs. The next morning, he brought this information to his neighbor and excitedly told him "I can't believe it! All these bills add up to ten percent of my income! I can't afford to not tithe!"

God will not lie, nor will His Word return to Him void. He asks His children to give him *only* ten percent of everything He gives us. Greed, fear, worries, and coveting causes us to make excuses to not tithe. But God told us fair and square what will happen if we rob Him. He will allow the devourer to take what was rightfully His. It shouldn't come as a shock. Your bills may not account for exactly ten percent as this man's did, it may be more since the devourer is not getting rebuked. Also, we want to express that not every time these expenses occur does it mean you are not tithing. God works in many ways. However, it is a large principle that needs constant checking.

It was not too hard to find our error in tithing as it was incredibly recent, and the Holy Spirit graciously brought to us these two particular areas where we robbed our God. One area was two payments from Luke's dad for $300: a simple tithe of thirty dollars out of each. Luke had rationalized that we had tithed on the income when we bought the supplies, so we didn't need to tithe the whole ten percent since we were only being paid back. Therefore, I tithed fifteen dollars both times. Not a big deal you say? If this habit of stealing, hence not trusting God for our provisions, was allowed to continue, it would most assuredly be inviting Satan in to pull us away from our relationship with our Father. We needed to put ourselves back under God's authority; back under His protection. You see, when we leave His authority we make ourselves vulnerable to Satan's attacks. Remember the fence (Chapter 9)? It's not to keep us in; it's to keep evil out.

We thanked our Father for showing us our iniquities since we ask to be taught of *God's* ways. We also thanked Him for opening the gate to receive us back into His authority. Remember these scriptures? Deuteronomy 8:5: "Thou shalt also consider in thine heart, that, as a man chasteneth his son, so the Lord thy God chasteneth thee." Hebrews 12:6 saying "For whom the Lord loveth he chasteneth, and scourgeth every son whom he receiveth." And how about Hebrews 12:7? "If ye endure chastening, God dealeth with you as with sons; for what son is he whom the father chasteneth not?"

Chastened, loved, and humbled at God's mercy, we went back to God. We are dependent on Christ's gift to us. Oh, how we need His blood to cover us. How thankful and loved we are to have a way to return home with God, to be forgiven. Ron Mehl (author of "*The Ten[der] Commandments*", page 253) said it right when he wrote:

"Some people outside of Christ think we're insane for putting our trust in the Bible and depending on the Lord Jesus the way we do. They say we're "emotional cripples" for having to lean on something outside ourselves. And to those comments I reply… *"Amen."* Absolutely. You want me to wear those labels? Hand 'em over and I'll put 'em on. I'm not ashamed to say there are days when I have *no idea* how I'm going to make it through. I am sustained and helped when I lean on the cross, when I lean on His Word. If leaning hard on God makes me handicapped in the eyes of the world, then bring on the wheelchair. I'm not ashamed to admit my TOTAL dependence upon Him."

We tithed what we owed and clarified again to tithe off the gross amounts of our earnings again since we had just recently begun tithing off profit only. We would not have that profit if the gross amount was not given and allowed by God. Understanding our errors, we were ready to be responsible for their consequences and pay the two-thousand dollars. We submitted this to God. The day before I was going to send in my paperwork, God laid it upon my heart to call the IRS. I called and explained, "I had sent in the 1099-R Form with my federal individual income tax return…"

"What's your SSN?" she said.

I gave it and tried again to fully explain myself when she interrupted with, "What tax year?"

"2007"

"And you have a 1099-R Form?"

"Yes" I answered

"Does it have a taxable amount on it?"

"No, but it does say it is the contributor's responsibility to figure this amount."

"You have a 1099-R Form and box two says zero? Send in the IRS response form marked you do not agree with any of the changes and send the 1099-R form with it" she was about to hang up as I hurriedly asked if I need to send in an amended tax form as I did fill out the taxes wrong (I was afraid of interest growing on the amount owed).

"No, just send in the two forms."

"Even though I sent in for the account history, and upon receiving it, I subtracted our total paid in contributions from the total distribution and came out with a difference of $181 in earnings? I still only send in those two forms?"

"Yes."

"So, I don't need to send in an amended return?"

She answered again to send in the Form and the Response. Well, thinking how much easier it would have been to just cheerfully tithe and suspecting the IRS of dragging this out just to collect more interest, I thanked the lady after taking her name and ID number and then recorded the whole conversation, names, date, and time of the call.

We thought how our omnipotent God can do anything. So, although we didn't deserve it, it was with hope of a merciful miracle that we mailed off the instructed forms and chose to not worry about the matter. We continued to thank our Father for His tender love and closeness to us that He should care enough to show us our wrongs and teach us. We thanked Him for His mercy and forgiveness, for His Son, for the chance to make our wrong into right. We praised His ability to take this matter away completely just as He brought it and we praised and humbly thanked Him for His provisions in this matter if we were to pay the total sum.

Two weeks later we were checking the mail when another IRS letter arrived. We quickly opened it with great anticipation. And it read: case closed. "Halleluiahs" rang out in the car echoed by more exuberant Halleluiahs by our children. Praises, thanks, and rejoicing led the way home and was reverently followed by earnest prayers at our family altar. That night another building stone of faith cured. The stone that was in the making was now finished and set in place. A new excitement in trusting our lives to God's control proceeded. How could we look at life the same after God so obviously showed His power?

In Deuteronomy 5:29 God is saying "O that there were such an heart in them, that they would fear me, and keep all my commandments always, that it might be well with them, and with their children for ever." Do you hear the tenderness and passion in this plea? God knows His children are going to stray from Him and He is hurting for them already, saying, "Please my beloved children, follow my rules so you won't hurt yourselves. I want to protect you, that's why I made these rules. *For you.* Trust my Words, give *me* your hearts." It is so exciting to belong to God!

In the end of April, we were blessed with the opportunity to spend a few weeks away from home to help family and friends. God had previously paid all our April bills and granted money for gas. Upon our return in May we went first to the post office. Luke came out with an envelope all blank but for our name and a stamp. We opened it to find forty dollars cash. Again, our vehicle rang with praises and exultations as we explained what happened to our children. Their eyes twinkled with excitement all the way home. It's only forty dollars, you say? No, it's much more than that. It is our loving Father presenting us with a gift. It's our Living God providing for us. It's a heavenly smile shining upon us. It's encouragement—shame on us if we allow even the smallest blessings to escape without rejoicing! Let us remember to not take anything for granted. If we don't acknowledge the little blessings, which in reality are not little, we ourselves may be blocking the way for larger blessings.

It was probably a week later when we received a phone call. A gentleman explained how he had called the city hall looking for someone to hire and Luke came highly recommended. Then, he proceeded to explain the job at hand. He had just bought a house here in Mullan and wanted everything in it torn out, the place gutted, and the lawn mowed. I recorded the address and relayed the information to Luke. When Luke checked the property to estimate a bid, he quoted him $150 plus dump fees.

"That isn't going to work, Luke..." Luke felt horrible that he overbid when on the phone he heard, "I'm going to give you $500 plus dump fees." Praise God!

Luke answered, "I don't know if you believe in God, but I think He sent you to me!" That weekend, our gentleman met Luke at his house and gave us an $800 check including dump fees. However, Luke found a man in town who collects all metals, and anything burnable can be dumped locally for free, and the dump fees were twenty dollars when $200 was accounted for. We were told to keep the extra! Halleluiah!

This same gentleman has been the vessel of heavenly blessings several times. We see God softening his heart toward Him and us, and we are exceedingly thankful.

There is another gentleman in town. And I say he is the sweetest man we have ever met. He is ninety years old and makes the most beautiful quilts I ever saw. He also is a willing vessel through whom God has provided for us. This gentleman would personally gift money to us. Although he did it himself, he did so in a quiet and secretive way. This avenue of giving was new to us. We felt like we were costing this dear man his resources, but he would graciously explain that God told him to do it and would not hear anything more. Wow! His generosity and boldness were inspirational and humbling.

One particular time I had a short talk with him confessing my awkwardness at receiving such blessings. We felt so unworthy. I was also worried he felt obligated or sorry for us. He said he was sorry for our feelings in the matter, and he didn't feel obligated at all. God had blessed him and laid it upon his heart to do something for us, and it was the only thing he knew to do. When he said: "it's good for me to do this," I understood. I told him I shall hereafter rejoice in his gifts and be blessed. In not cheerfully and thankfully receiving his gifts, we were about to steal his blessing of giving.

This man gives us something else, too. He gives us a godly example to uphold before our children. I thank God for putting him into our path, because finding such joyful servants of God are rare. This model of generously giving and being glad to do so makes my heart sing that my children get to witness it. We love this sweet gentleman very dearly, and not for his money, but for the spirit that lives in his heart. He will be a living illustration to help sculpt our children's hearts and spirits.

I will never get tired of hearing or telling about God's wondrous works. He has been everything to us. How then could we ever stop talking about Him? So many miracles, and such an abundance of mercy and grace given by our Good Father. "There is none good but one, that is, God..." (Matthew 19:17) We are but dust. God *is* Good. No, God is *great*! How we love to belong to Him. With Him we are home.

CHAPTER 14

Will a Cloth hold us back?

I hardly feel qualified to write this chapter, but here it goes…
One day when Luke and I were reading our Bibles, Luke came over to the couch, where I sat. He asked if he could read a chapter to me. He read 1Corinthians, chapter eleven, verses one through sixteen:

> "Be ye followers of me, even as I also am of Christ.
>
> Now I praise you, brethren, that ye remember me in all things, and keep the ordinances, as I delivered them to you.
>
> But I would have you know, that the head of every man is Christ; and the head of the woman is the man; and the head of Christ is God.
>
> Every man praying or prophesying, having his head covered, dishonoreth his head.
>
> But every woman that prayeth or prophesieth with her head uncovered dishonoreth her head: for that is even all one as if she were shaven.

For if the woman be not covered, let her also be shorn: but if it be a shame for a woman to be shorn or shaven, let her be covered.

For a man indeed ought not to cover his head, forasmuch as he is the image and glory of God: but the woman is the glory of the man.

For the man is not of the woman; but the woman of the man.

Neither was the man created for the woman; but the woman for the man.

For this cause ought the woman to have power on her head because of the angels.

Nevertheless neither is the man without the woman, neither the woman without the man, in the Lord.

For as the woman is of the man, even so is the man also by the woman; but all things of God.

Judge in yourselves: is it comely that a woman pray unto God uncovered?

Doth not even nature itself teach you, that, if a man have long hair, it is a shame unto him?

But if a woman have long hair, it is a glory to her: for her hair is given her for a covering.

But if any man seem to be contentious, we have no such custom, neither the churches of God."

As he read I knew where he was headed. Memories of the few women I've seen in head coverings flashed before me: somber faces, joyless countenances, almost fear or shame to look at anyone else, and a purposeful oblivion to anyone else in the world. I burst into tears and cried. I cried because I thought it would make me joyless and I would have to be like them. I cried because I thought nobody would want to talk to me. I cried because I thought people would look at me weirdly. I cried because it seemed the last thread of normalcy I had with the world. Then I cried because I couldn't cheerfully comply with *anything* God asked of me. I also cried at the obvious vanity in my heart. I cried from grief, not anger. It was a silly, immature reaction because my heart felt it was right, but my flesh wasn't willing.

I really *wanted* to obey God's dress code if that is how He views modesty for His children. I have lived and seen God's love first hand enough to covet more of it. I want to immerse myself and my children in His love, and if the only thing God was asking of me was to wear a piece of cloth on my head, then how hard could that be? My spirit was thankful for something to do for my Father after He had done so much for us. But, my flesh was at war.

I poured out my heart to Luke, and he was very sympathetic as we began to study this chapter and others. The more we chose to openly look upon these scriptures without influences and ask God to show us *His* truth, the more it seemed a positive thing. At first, though, the man-made headings were a hang-up for me. Man put above these 1 Corinthian verses "public worship". If ever there was bait for an excuse, this was it, and I gladly swallowed it whole. It provided me with a way out—a poor way. For my flesh, I put man's word above God's inspired Word.

I wavered back and forth between it meaning public worship or all the time. Luke gently informed me that he felt it meant all the time, but he was not going to command me to wear it. He wanted my heart to be at peace with it, and I didn't have to wear it until I was ready to. I told him I believe wearing a head-covering to church or Bible studies were right. The benefits were plentiful. When we go to the house of God, it needs to be *completely* about God. Not our hair types, not our hair-styles, not even spending the time to arrange our hair vainly, etc. They served as a modesty tool to keep all awareness on God. So, we began wearing head-coverings during these occasions. It turned out to be a blessing to be in attendance and not have praises for worthless things. For example: Nyomi's hair. God gave her wavy brown ringlets, and this brings a lot of attention. Therefore, when we are in God's house to worship *Him*, it felt wrong to have the attraction on her hair.

Soon after this, the Holy Spirit pressed my heart asking, "Why not all the time?" You know, the only answer I could come up with was "what would other people think?" I would then make excuses: "my head couldn't breathe, it would be unhealthy for my hair," or "I could no longer witness for God because people would think I'm too weird." But these excuses served to only build-up my faith that wearing them was right, as God allowed me to see the pure vanity behind them. I even asked God to reveal another example in the Bible that demonstrates His children wore them. I found Numbers 5:18 and Isaiah chapter forty-seven. In the book of *Numbers*, a priest uncovered a woman's head, thus exemplifying they did indeed wear coverings. In Isaiah 47:2-3, God illustrates the Babylonian women's immodesty when He says: "…uncover thy locks, make bare the leg, uncover the thigh, pass over the rivers. [3] Thy nakedness shall be uncovered, yea, thy shame shall be seen…" Covering the hair is woven together with modesty here. Our flesh and attributes, which glorify women, are treasures to be saved for our husbands and not bared for the world.

I'll share a few things we learned concerning the following verses:

"But I would have you know, that the head of every man is Christ; and the head of the woman is the man; and the head of Christ is God." Clearly, there is an order of authority being re-established here.

"Every man praying or prophesying, having his head covered, dishonoreth his head." When a man witnesses, prays, etc. he discredits himself by wearing a covering over his head. Pretty simple. So why was it confusing to me when it read the opposite way?

"But every woman that prayeth or prophesieth with her head uncovered dishonoreth her head: for that is even all one as if she were shaven." There is a distinction being made between the last verse and this. A woman who witnesses or prays, etc. is dishonoring her head if she is not veiled. Other words for dishonor are degradation, scandal, public disgrace, shameful, discredit, and disgrace. She brings these on herself, and on her authority, if not modestly and appropriately covered. I have been told that this only applied to their culture and our culture is different today. To this I say, "I don't want to be like our world's culture, I **want** God's culture!" The majority of women in today's society would also agree that shaving their head bald would be embarrassing. This scripture links having a shaven head the same as being uncovered. Shouldn't then, it be the same today? Shouldn't we be embarrassed at not having our hair veiled? Is not covering our hair like telling God that we WILL be equal with man in His chain of command?

"For if the woman be not covered, let her also be shorn: but if it be a shame for a woman to be shorn or shaven, let her be covered." This explains the choice for women to have in appearance: the shamefulness of being shorn, or, to wear a covering.

"For a man indeed ought not to cover his head, forasmuch as he is the image and glory of God: but the woman is the glory of the man." Why doesn't man cover his head? Because he is the image and glory of God. Why do women need to cover their heads? Because

they are the glory of man. God is showing us diversity of man and woman. I believe it helps us remember how we were made and what for; a living banner that proclaims submission to God's chain of command in the face of the world and in opposition to feminism. It is a helpful reminder of the organization of God. Everything is for a purpose. And knowing God has a reason, I want to obey the slightest implication. At this verse, it actually sounds quite clear. Women veil their hair to show their obedience to God's rank of authority. God set it in order and we get to be living illustrations of His creation.

"For the man is not of the woman; but the woman of the man." Again, here is another reason why this distinction is made. Women were first created from the man's rib, not independently created.

"Neither was the man created for the woman; but the woman for the man." The head-covers are symbolic of creation. It's very nature to wear one puts your creation-purpose right before your eyes. It's a constant accountability. It is one more helpful tool provided to women to remain in their roles, to be a helpmeet as God created you to be.

"For this cause ought the woman to have power on her head because of the angels." This one is the pounding sentence proclaimed. The head-coverings are a symbol and a sign even to the angels of your acknowledgement of the chain of command set in motion by God and portrays your heart in serving and playing out your part.

"Nevertheless neither is the man without the woman, neither the woman without the man, in the Lord." Here is the comfort that, although

there is a clear difference between men and women's roles, we are all equally welcome to God.

"For as the woman is of the man, even so is the man also by the woman; but all things of God." Woman was indeed created out of man, but we mutually need each other as shows the full circle of life: man is born out of woman. But all things remain in organized ranking.

"Judge in yourselves: is it comely that a woman pray unto God uncovered?" Paul tells us to judge ourselves of what was such a common, normal understanding of God's people. Luke's judgment was clear to me. My judgment is that I want to please God because I love Him and do not wish to pervert His authority arrangement by making myself as a man, usurping my true headship. God wants me to follow my husband and be under his authority. I felt that being able to cheerfully comply with a minor thing would honor God as well as my husband. I know God was with me before I wore head coverings, but I now had new knowledge and could not seem to shake awkwardness when fellowshipping, sharing scriptures, and praying (which we are to do unceasingly). Not for legalism's sake, but I could no longer expect God to wink at me in ignorance. I had new knowledge and needed to live it. I began to think "how can I be a witness if I don't submit and follow God?" So, I may not understand all the whys but my heart has experienced the blessings of obedience first, we can understand later. Nowhere in scripture will you find "understand first, and then follow my instruction". Out of *faith*, we follow God's total inspired Word, and someday we will understand.

"Doth not even nature itself teach you, that, if a man have long hair, it is a shame unto him?"

"But if a woman have long hair, it is a glory to her: for her hair is given her for a covering." Is a woman's hair her covering, as in a head-cover? If it is, then why would God give the ultimatum earlier about being shaven or covered? If your hair was indeed the cover, then you would have the choice to have shaven hair or long hair. But that wasn't what **God** said. He said shorn or covered. And shall one verse nullify all previous twelve verses? We decided to get several varying Bible versions out and compare these passages. The newer they got, the more this verse seemed the exception to the rule, a compromise. It provided women in today's culture an easy way out. Once I read this, I felt even stronger that God's ways were the opposite. And, what if our long hair *is* our glory? We have many other womanly attributes that are our glory as well and we don't get to flaunt those openly. They remain hidden treasures and a glory reserved for our husbands. Is the hair any different?

"But if any man seem to be contentious, we have no such custom, neither the churches of God." My footnotes (which are frequently wrong) say Paul was demonstrating that 'like it or not, this is the way it is.' Here is not a tradition, but a living principle. To question this moral practice, Paul counted you as contentious.

So, now you have our thoughts on the subject. Why do I wear a cover? First, because I love God and find it a joy to follow His Word, at the expense of being peculiar to the world, if it pleases Him. The second reason I wear one is because I love my husband. God asks me to submit to my husband "as if he were God." And Luke does like me to wear a veil.

Scripture really seems to encourage women to cover their hair, outwardly showing the heart's surrender to God's wonderful order. It comes down to faith in His plan. Is it a sin against God to not wear one? I suppose that depends completely on the heart. I, perhaps being an elbow in the body of Christ, cannot rightfully make the decisions for the arm, or the head. Paul says to judge yourselves. I want you to understand *my* wickedness here. All I was asked to do was wear a little material on my head. Before I could comply with that *small* request, I had to ask God's help to pull the weeds in my heart because my identity was still wrapped in the world. It was literally baby steps. For a really short time, my insecurities put up a wall between other people, and I thought for sure they were condemning me when they looked at me. I found my heart was terribly rebellious. I was embarrassed to be God's child because of a cloth. His Word says if we are ashamed of Him, then He will be ashamed of us in the end. God is so patient! He helped me see how I had put chains on myself because of a bit of fabric. He helped to unlock those chains and set me free.

We are no scholars of the Word, but this is our best understanding so far. And for me, my ultimate understanding is to follow the voices of the ones I love (who also are ordained to be my guides). The head-coverings are now a part of my clothing and I am *free* to talk and mingle with joy among all people. God has even graciously put other women, who veil their hair, into my path who are full of life, vitality and God's love. What a joy it is to fellowship with them.

As long as I get to toss my mane around for my husband, then I am happy. I no longer need the world to affirm me. I want my identity as God's child, no matter how much it defies culture. Will a piece of cloth hold me back? It did once. And once again, God loves us and helps us through the fire so we can have faith fit for heaven. Will a piece of cloth hold you back? It may not be a head-covering; it may be some other small thing that we tend to denounce God for. Thank you, God, for having the keys to free us from our chains!

CHAPTER 15

A Transplant, If You Please

Year 2009 held three vital themes which God used to further train us. One was *unity*, unity as we meshed our hearts to God's Holy Scriptures and His perfect timing. This past year has also been significant in teaching us how to function as a biblical family. But first, we needed God to remove the links to our past. When these chains fell and we were free, it enabled new building blocks of love and faith for our family to connect our hearts and hands through every aspect in life. Our marriage made some important breakthroughs as well. As a married couple, a deeper bond of unity has been realized, making us closer than ever before.

Our second theme is *faith*. Although it is security to understand God is in control and capable of everything, I am weak too often and have too little faith. But we will not make it into an excuse. We get to continue our path of learning to gain, gain, gain, and we gain for God's magnificent glory as He long suffers us. Jesus told his disciples "...for verily I say unto you, If ye have faith as a grain of mustard seed (did you catch that, just a grain!), ye shall say unto this mountain, Remove hence to yonder place; and it shall remove;

and nothing shall be impossible unto you." (Matthew 17:20) Who can boast such a thing? Indeed, we cannot! Hebrews 11:1 reads "Now faith is the substance of things hoped for, the evidence of things not seen." When we understand something and carry it out, then we show wisdom. When we do not understand and perform from obedience, we use faith: trusting and believing God.

The third theme of year 2009 is *dependence*. It was pretty obvious that each bill paid was by God's money. Every job offered to Luke was a heavenly provision. When everything we have is God's (or from God through other avenues) it really emphasizes our dependence upon our Heavenly Father. Something I wouldn't change at all since our peace and protection is in the joyful dependence upon our Lord.

What a glorious year it has been! As we learned these crucial values of submitting one's whole life to *God's* will, we found comfort, security, and happiness to be the consequences. Following God *always* ends in victory so we don't have to be scared. Being scared is faithless and not fun, but trusting God will always be an exciting adventure.

The summer of 2009 brought something else: a request from David Munsen to his sons to donate a portion of their liver to him. You see, the only thing left for him was a transplant, death, or divine healing. David obviously did not like death as an option and thus asked his sons to consider becoming a live-liver-donor, as they had the best chance to match his own liver type. This procedure would require major surgery to remove sixty percent of the donor's liver and transplant it into the recipient's body after discarding the diseased liver. The liver, being regenerative, would grow back to their original sizes for both. I am not writing about the transplant itself, even though both Luke and his dad are alive and well today. God brought them both through surgery with flying colors and in the shortest recovery times allowed. This story *is* a wonderful miracle, especially as Luke did not believe in these procedures at first, but I do not wish to write about the progressive thinking that led my husband into making his decisions. There is too much involved and too much at stake for the sake of others to share any details of family thoughts, feelings, and lessons. These must be kept private between God and ourselves. The whole surgery is to God's credit and praises forever!

God graciously arranged for our entire family to accompany Luke to Arizona for his operation. Although the option was open for quite some time, it was not until the end when the decision was made honestly and adamantly by my husband. What a glorious break-through! In the course of a few trials, God transplanted fresh views to replace Luke's youthful observations and examples. I had been praying about these factors for our relationship for years! I can't mark exactly why or when the transplant happened, but I wish it to remain between Luke and God. I am only too glad to bask in my new husband! One might think this is an exaggeration. However, without this transplant of the heart for Luke, the outcome of several various situations during the liver transplant would not be the same. The scope of the nearing surgery was that extensive; the surgery itself being just a fragment in the events. From this turning point, Luke and I shared a new closeness. I love the scripture "Behold, I stand at the door, and knock: if any man hear my voice, and open the door, I will come into him, and will sup with him, and he with me" (Revelation 3:20). So many areas in our lives need to be conformed. This cannot happen until we answer the knock and invite our Lord Jesus Christ in. Even though we may try and try, the restoration will not occur until we submit to our Lord and commit to His ways. Only then can our *garden* be correctly transformed.

Everywhere we are and in everything we do it is our first responsibility to honor God. This time in our lives was no different. September 8th, 2009, our family, along with Larry Sendelbach, as main caregiver for Luke, boarded the plane for Phoenix, Arizona. We settled into our hotel, and I selfishly planned on a private vacation with the family, concentrating on our children and my husband. Although this specific aspect didn't change, God had plans for a bigger picture. And what an artist He is!

As we met several hotel patrons, we began to notice the ministry opportunities God was opening up. It was so much fun to reach out to others and show them God's love and glory! Right away we felt like we were in the midst of a family reunion! Many people were attracted by the love shining in our children's' eyes, the smiles they freely gave everyone, and by their respectable behavior. Through our children, God brought a multitude of visitors and fellowship opportunities. With excitement, we witnessed, shared testimonies, told of God's love, encouraged, and watched God open and effect hearts. We looked forward to those breakfasts which lasted two or three hours with the eating and all the fellowshipping. It was great! God was teaching us how our time is never our own, at least not if we truly desire to live and serve Him. And we do want this above *all* else! I wouldn't want it any other way. Our lives are God's, to be used any way He wishes. Living selfishly, only concerned about our own affairs isn't fun like it is to always be open to others, constantly ready to spread God's love and saving Words. The very fact that God was willing to use us broken vessels was a blessing of blessings! By the third day God had created a close family atmosphere. He gave others a sense of comfort with us that enabled them to open their hearts, sorrows and pain. And we received the blessings of watching first-hand how God held them as they spoke and we listened, how He comforted and gave hope through loving touches, biblical encouragement; showing His love for them and their situation, and prayer. Larry experienced an outreach ministry above this as he became an active supportive member for other families during their surgeries. God is so great! We are very thankful for this amazing time. The friendships quickly created were bonded so closely that we had several people praying over Luke and his dad and shedding tears over our family.

Another reminder God brought to our family in these days was the importance of true character. One of the hardest situations in life is treating your own family with the same respect and love that you would give to others. It's almost too easy to extend a quick helping hand to someone else who smiles and exhibits gratitude, to feel important in tending their needs, sharing their joys, or politely listen. How often do we find it a burden to speak the same kind, endearing words to our household members, to extend the servant's hands in the same joyfulness and humble attentiveness in support of our family? It is much harder. We don't receive the same gratitude. Our family knows our flaws, sins, and hypocrisies. This can be hard to forgive in itself. I am so thankful that God continues to remind us of the importance of genuine character (what you do and who you are when nobody else is around). Who we are should not differ from one circumstance to the next.

You have heard it said 'trials refine us'. But, also, really, 'trials reveal us.' Our character is not how we act on the outside; it's what spills out from the inside. When we Christians are squeezed in life, Jesus needs to come out and not everything else. For our children's souls, we must show God's love and glory to them in the same manner we are willing to be there for others. Our children will exemplify the inward character we really hold. We need to wash in the blood of Christ and accept the forgiveness to ourselves for the shortcomings in parenting, living, and loving, as well as forgive our family of theirs. Just as God long suffers patiently for us, we need to duplicate this toward ours. Practice seeing your family members through God's eyes and not our fleshly eyes which remember injustices. I am grateful that God will help me compare my fellowshipping with strangers to my fellowshipping with husband and children. Their souls are most important. I don't want to teach them hypocrisy. I don't want them to feel like mama enjoys strangers more than I enjoy them. Wherever I am and with whomever I'm with, I want to be consistent for God's glory.

God was so close to us during this entire process! Miles and miles from home, He was still our Teacher, our Guide, our Advisor, our Comforter, our Physician, and yes, our abundant Provider. This surgery required Luke to have very little income the month preceding the operation and the months during and after the operation. We entrusted this to God. Several times during the qualifying process we had not earned enough to meet our coming bills. Nevertheless, we patiently waited for God knowing He wouldn't forsake us, and He always provided. Yes, our gracious Father always provides when we seek Him first (Matthew chapter 6)! We persevered in remembering "God's work first, always God first."

Before our bills were due, one unexpected avenue after another portrayed God's caring guardianship. A $2,000 check from one source came a month before the surgery date. Hundreds appeared in a variety of other ways, too. In Arizona, all the expenses were paid for. When we came home in October, God had put the desire to provide on our neighbors. This was completely unexpected! I love God's surprises! It feels like a great big hug! Full turkey dinners, roasts, potatoes, vegetables, and fruit set us up for several weeks. Mom, Grandma and Grandpa, and Aunt Kris, provided more grocery and meal items while Nicki and Dave and David provided gas money for visiting as well. Have you ever felt like crying under the continuous blessings being showered upon you? It was so much from God, to us!

The provisions didn't stop there. God had more power He wanted to show us. We soon learned of a letter arriving with monetary help. This family heard of the situation and God touched their hearts toward us. Through them, whom we've only met once, God bestowed $1,000. In December, Luke had begun to work part-time, but during this month we received a phone call announcing a gift held for us. We, overwhelmed and humbled, went to see what God had planned. After visiting, we left with an envelope. At home we opened our heavenly gift to see $1,000 in cash. Oh, magnificent Father! How great Thou art! Infinitely beautiful is Your love!

Both His lessons and trials have become equally beautiful to us. How could they not be? We understand these trials are just as much out of love and for our good as the other blessings, miracles, and provisions. To receive guidance and chastisement from our God is the biggest blessing of all. He does it because He counts us His children. Someday He will call His children home to Him. Home, sweet home! Doesn't this make you want to do *anything* and *everything* to have such love and security of a truly dependable Father? Doesn't this magnify your love for God? Doesn't this make living by His Holy Scriptures so very worth it? We love to be in God's will and obey His Words. We love to live in such freedom and adventure by seeking after our Living God.

When we closed out our finances for year 2009, we were gifted almost $7,000. God grossed $11,000 to us through our earned income. We had such an abundant year! Never were we even close to being "in need." If we felt we needed or wanted something, we would share it with God and leave it with Him. It's not our flesh we want controlling us, it's God's plan. If our desires are actual needs, we know God will grant it one way or another. If He doesn't want to gratify that desire, for whatever reason, then we don't want it either. Our will is that God's will be done. After Jesus gave His life to us for God, it is a small thing to live our lives serving Him. After all, there is proof enough of the benefits directly attached to following God's commands. Such security, freedom, and truth is found nowhere else than living under the Bible's authority, seeking after God and His Son.

We hope and pray you will ask and allow God to come into your life and give you a heart, mind, and soul transplant. Ask Him continually to conform your ways to His, for it *is* a continual process. Become one of His children. Experience being born again, and share in the heavenly chorus of our redemption story.

CHAPTER 16

Josiah Ray Munsen

~ Born March 2010 ~

In July 2009 our family took a trip to view a twenty-acre piece of property in Fruitland, Washington, near Springdale. Our friends Larry and Jan live close to this piece, and Larry had previewed it for us upon our interest. On this day, Larry was with us as companion and tour guide to the property which was surrounded by state land and priced at $35,000.

Although I cannot recall what topic of conversation brought us to talking of our children, it came nonetheless. As I was speaking of our five children, Larry turned to look back at me with a puzzled expression. When I again mentioned "five" kids he turned, counted, and asked, "You mean four?" I gave him a very curious look wondering why he would be questioning me about such a thing as I should know how many kids I have. I quickly glanced around the suburban and confirmed "five" with a nod of my head.

"Is there something you haven't told me yet?"

Now confused at this odd puzzlement, I proceeded to point to each child in the car and count out loud. When I came to four, I turned back to Larry and answered "four" as if that was what I had said all along. Seeing that I still did not understand the dilemma, Larry explained I was saying "five" each time. Suddenly, it all came to my realization that I had indeed claimed five children quite adamantly.

"So, is there something I don't know?" He asked again laughing.

Laughing myself, I countered "not that I know of yet."

"Well, maybe God is *trying* to tell you something! Or, if you're not pregnant now, then you may be soon!"

What an exciting idea and what a wonderful way to find out! Thus, knowledge of our fifth pregnancy began. God told us before any symptoms or signs appeared. In fact, it was more than a month until we confirmed what God knew. When we called to tell the "official" confirmation to Larry and Jan, they said they weren't surprised as they had figured we were since that drive. How exciting to serve our God! What a blessed start to a new pregnancy and life, to have such proof that God was there from the beginning.

Nothing unusual occurred during the prenatal care. Rather than consuming vitamins, my nutritional needs were met solely through proper diet. This was accomplished by following our Holy Spirit's promptings for any extra nutrition needed and what foods or herbs to get them through. I felt healthy the entire duration of the pregnancy and we exceedingly praise God for it all! I don't ever want to take good health for granted, as I have experienced the other side of it. How very thankful I am! Through my fifth pregnancy, I still have never experienced morning sickness, but I have always undergone bouts of exhaustion. This time was no different. In fact, during the third trimester, taking a nap and/or lying down to rest became a daily routine.

I remember one week a growth spurt developed so suddenly, that my body did not have time to grow with it. That week resulted in lying down the majority of the time because it caused pain to walk around. My muscles and ligaments were not strong enough to support such rapid growth yet. When I did walk (or hobble) I leaned forward to take the weight off my ligaments. This helped a lot, but caused severe back aches and pain. Thus, the best thing I could do was simply rest until my body caught up. Sure enough, a week later the back pain quit and I could walk in proper posture quite normally and pain free.

This time did not seem hard in any way as our children are wonderful helpers. They performed the tasks and duties that I could not—and voluntarily at that. I would no sooner lie down on the couch when one of them (Prudence included) would be covering me up with a blanket. Then they would happily finish their chores. What a blessing to be so taken care of! Luke was great, too. He was my personal masseuse, warding off the aches and fighting the pain with his strong capable hands, stopping whatever he was doing to offer his assistance when needed. He wouldn't just throw a massage together, either. He diligently massaged deep and well for an hour. Every time, the therapy would put me back into working order, and after a tiny nap, I would be restored to health. I sing praises of thankfulness to God for my husband! Just as God has changed me, He has blossomed Luke into a husband and father that words of gratitude can't describe. And I get to forever sing my song of praises to our Heavenly Teacher.

About thirty-two weeks along (Sunday, February 14) I had a day of painful and continuous contractions. Premature labor entered our minds and we made two phone calls for prayer and sought our Great Physician as a family as well. This could have been an excuse to worry or get scared, but we were confident in God's power and purpose for everything. He alone could take care of it, and we trusted to His will and timing. The following day began immediately with several hard contractions and back pain which continued into the afternoon. I remained on the couch the entire morning, drinking lots of water. That afternoon God stayed the labor and everything returned to normal. At thirty-three weeks we had two more days of strong Braxton-hicks, and our baby dropped quite noticeably. This resulted in nothing more than space to eat, breathe, and slouch.

Thirty-five weeks gestation marked the occasion all of us girls went to Grandma's for a week's rest and vacation, and to break up the routine for the boys before the new baby arrived. Mom picked us up in town Monday, and we had a lovely time all week. The boys visited Grandpa David and worked with Luke a few days before joining us at Mom's on Thursday night for the remainder of the week until Sunday. The week during our stay and the next week upon our return, normalcy reigned with naps, contractions, and walks.

Saturday, March 20th, at 4:25am I awoke with an intense contraction that sent a flush up to my shoulders at its end.

"Today, huh?" I asked God, and after a peaceful minute I followed with the thoughtful confirmation that "today's going to be the day."

I was very thankful that God changed my plans the previous Thursday into finishing all baby preparations. That day all the baskets and beds were prepared. Blankets and birthing room were ready for immediate use. I had also vacuumed the suburban to buckle in the infant car seat. So, that Saturday morning, which marked thirty-seven weeks, I remained in bed to relax or sleep as I wished. Irregularly, about every fifteen to thirty minutes, another labor contraction would come. I was completely at peace with labor taking place that day. It never seemed to be wrong. As I lay there talking with my beloved God, it felt as though three angels stood bedside. We were taken care of. God had us guarded and protected. That's all we needed.

At six o'clock I got up to make some juice and start the heater in the birth room. When Luke appeared I asked him how a baby sounded today. With him smiling, I recounted the morning and we settled in for a birth. Breakfast and Bible readings followed. About 10:30am we went for a hard walk. Contractions had been no longer than twelve minutes apart the whole morning, although irregular. During the walk they came two and a-half minutes apart strictly, slowing after the walk ended. Eleven o'clock we all took our naps and the contractions stayed about fifteen minutes apart, not overly painful, but working and stretching. Half past noon found intensity picking up. We ended the nap at 12:45 and Luke began dinner for the family. I mentioned to him that it won't be long before I'll want the pool filled. Only a little while later, with several contractions three minutes apart, I changed my mind and informed him I needed the pool filled now just in case. So, he juggled dinner preparations, filling the pool, and heating water while I meandered about inside and outside with the children.

This labor was very calm and peacefully slow. It wouldn't have surprised me if things continued into Sunday because hard labor seemed so far away. Luke declared that he thought every labor was getting easier and easier. I laughed at him but wondered at the simplicity and calm, contented atmosphere the whole day held. Even with contractions two to three minutes apart, it seemed so relaxed! I agreed with Luke at how strange this birth was.

I had no feelings of wanting the hot pool water. We praised God for His care and help, and I decided to try taking a nap. I soon became bored. Therefore, I thought I might as well use the pool since it was filled. Therefore, Nyomi and I headed downstairs to the birth room, she with her coloring and me with my fluids.

Although contractions continued, I no longer timed them. My water still had not broken—an answered prayer. Probably an hour later, I became impatient and told Luke, who had come down to spend time with me that I thought I'd again try to nap. Luke chuckled and said, "This is really weird; you don't seem to be in labor at all!" And he praised God for supporting me.

I settled with all my pillows on the bed. I did not sleep, but deeply relaxed for several contractions when one hit that warned me of transition. I knew things would no longer be "fun." I lay there through three and decided the weightlessness of the pool suddenly sounded good. Nyomi radioed Luke and announced the contractions were closer together now. Luke said he would return to check on me. He showed up and watched through two more before needing to leave. He no sooner reached the top of the stairs when everything came *hard* and fast. I instructed Nyomi to radio Luke and notify him that "it's time." She quickly got the walkie-talkie and screamed to Luke, "Mama's in labor! Daddy, Mama's in labor!!" Luke came right back for the crescending five minutes of birth. All at once, the familiar deep welling of transition intensity hit with one contraction immediately after another. I cried aloud for God to give me strength for what was to come, and as expected, our baby was quickly and safely born.

With a deep sigh of thankfulness that it was done and a rush of adrenaline, I picked up our baby. He softly cried for a minute, but stopped when I talked to him, then opened his eyes and began to look around. He even tilted his chin up to look about him and his eyes moved side to side just taking everything in. We checked, and indeed, it was a boy!

Luke got the warm towels to cover our baby boy. Nyomi and I glowed over the birth and our baby while I relaxed. After Luke returned, he cut the cord, as it was white. We all went upstairs where our other children loved and talked of how cute their newborn baby was. Later, Luke weighed him in a gown to be seven pounds and half an ounce, so we called him seven pounds even.

Over the course of the pregnancy, we favored two names for a boy: Josiah and Honour. As time passed it seemed Josiah was his name and choosing Honour actually felt like we were changing his name. Thus, our son became Josiah Ray Munsen, carrying my dad's middle name.

The following morning we measured Josiah to be 19 ½ inches long with 13 ½ inches around his head. Again, I was carried through birth without any tears or lacerations at all! And, there wasn't any extra bleeding! We deeply and humbly bow before our God for His care and mercies, and for allowing us to birth in such a fashion. Worthy is our Great Physician, our Sovereign Father in Heaven!

The last thing God prepared us for was the necessity for a long recovery. I thought it would be hard to make myself nap, rest, and stay in bed or inactive. But God knows best! As it turned out, the rest was extremely welcomed and required. I could not figure out why I felt the need to sleep and take extra fluids or why my energy seemed low. It was about three days later my body passed a large clot. Afterwards, my energy jumped and I walked easier. But I still carried on with the recovery plan. The next day a few more large clots passed and after each one a boost of energy and vitality arrived. I was now feeling absolutely great! I continued Tuesday through Thursday confined to my room to rest, write, and recover. For weeks after I still lifted nothing more than Josiah out of respect for my recovery and long term health. The second week post-birth, as I became more active, my prolapse became a concern. My muscles were still too weak and not ready for full activity. So, I took it easy for another few weeks and we prayed much over it. God heard our petition and granted healing soon thereafter.

Josiah was so healthy, strong, and alert at birth, he was every bit full term to us. If I could find anything to pin prematurity on him, it would be his breathing. He would breathe fast and shallow. We had learned many births ago about "Kangaroo Care." It is the practice of carrying your baby with you. This has been proven to quickly develop premature babies, and soothe colicky babies, affording longer and more restful sleep. A mother's chest will naturally change temperature to either heat up baby, maintain, or cool down. This helps the baby to better use his energy in growing rather than creating heat for himself. Well, we proved this idea first-hand. When he was only a little ways away, Josiah would continue his quick breaths. Conversely, when I held him on my chest he would immediately begin to breathe deeply and become relaxed. At night, it was the same thing. If he laid next to me on his own, his rapid breaths proceeded, so I would tuck him in close to me, swaddled in his blankets, and he slept soundly and peacefully.

With gladness, we turn all glory toward God, the true Deliverer of our babies and souls!

I end this chapter with the poem I wrote
to commemorate Josiah's birth:

The Time of Life is Here Again
~scriptures borrowed from Psalm 127 & 128~
~poem by Roxanne Munsen~

"Lo, children are a heritage of the Lord…"
Into this vision our life we have poured.
For when He says "the fruit of the womb is His reward,"
It's with thankfulness that ALL His blessings will be stored.
Maintaining a vision for a multigenerational plan,
Our children will be "as arrows in the hand of a mighty man."
"Happy is the man that hath his quiver full of them,"
And to this faithful piece of wisdom, I say "AMEN!"

But God did not give us a quiver to only hold four,
If "children shall be like olive plants round
the table", there have to be more!
As a blessing He said "thy wife shall
be a fruitful vine" & thrive,
So, he created life and now we have five.
God said "Behold, thus shall a man be
blessed who fears the Lord"
To pass on a godly heritage with the cutting of the cord.
Oh, how mercifully and gracious Your best gifts You bestow,
To entrust to us a soul that Your kingdom may grow.

CHAPTER 17

Deliverance

The sensation of freedom is most appreciated by those who knew they have been bound. I am so thankful we have the Truth to set us free from ourselves. "Self" is a black hole, always resulting in your wanting more, never leaving you completely fulfilled. Our beloved Jesus expressed that "If ye continue in my word *then* are ye my disciples indeed. And ye shall know the truth and the truth shall make you free" (John 8:31-36). Continuing in His word is how we 'submit [ourselves] to God to resist the devil so he will flee from us' (James 4:7). "Whosoever committeth sin is the servant of sin." "Ye shall die in your sins, for if ye believe not that I am He, ye shall die in your sins" (John 8:24). How then do the bonds release? "For God so loved the world that He gave His only begotten Son, that whosoever believeth in Him should not perish, but have everlasting life. For God sent not His Son into the world to condemn the world; but that the world, through Him, might be saved. He that believeth on Him is not condemned: but He that believeth not is condemned already, because he hath not believed in the name of the only begotten Son of God. And this is the condemnation, that light is come into the world, and men loved darkness rather than light, because their deeds were evil. For every one that doeth evil hateth the light, neither cometh to the light, lest his deeds should be reproved. But he that doeth truth cometh to the light, that his deeds may be made manifest, that they are wrought in God" (John 3:16-21).

The keys to freedom are in His truthful words. Thank you, Jesus, for your love, your obedience, your encouraging words, and for performing your Father's Will as you said in John 6:40-58: "And this is the Will of Him that sent me, that every one which seeth the Son, and believeth on Him, may have everlasting life: and I will raise him up at the last day…Verily, verily, I say unto you, He that believeth on me hath everlasting life…and I will raise him up at the last day. For my flesh is meat indeed, and my blood is drink indeed. He that eateth my flesh, and drinketh my blood, dwelleth in me, and I in him."

The opportunity of freedom did indeed come when our beloved Jesus Christ gave up His life for the lives of the world upon that cross. Our deliverance is now at hand and we shall soon meet our Creator! How exciting! And what a fun adventure it is, striving to live after His word.

We have also been blessed to be delivered in an earthly sense as well. As you know, we had repented of buying a house through debt, and decided to sell it. We listed our home on some free real estate websites, craiglist.org, and the "Multiple Listings Service," too. Rather than lose a six percent commission of the purchase price, we opted to buy a flat fee listing. This meant, for a few hundred dollars, our property and house was listed on the MLS, and we still worked as our own agents as "For Sale by Owner." The interesting results were that only one viewing of our house occurred through the MLS, all others were by alternative routes. Some arrived by accident, having been searching for something else and God kindly routed their "lostness" to our street where they saw our sign in the yard. Others came after seeing our signs in the post office.

I would surmise the toughest aspect of selling our home was our decision to be flexible and present the property instantly if need be. Hence, we kept it cleaned, staged, and ready twenty-four-seven. Since all our viewings were sudden, this plan, although hard during slow times, definitely paid off in the end. When a car slowly drove by or pulled up, the children knew exactly what to do. Upon the announcement that "someone's here!" they immediately scrambled around and within five minutes had the floors clear, beds made, and rooms cleaned. We always showed our visitors the outside property, garage, and shed first. Then, upon entering the house, it was ready, too, thanks to the children.

Well, it was about one and a half years before our house sold. Not a terrible wait, but we were impatient several times since nothing was selling around us either. It was that last winter when a car drove by. Not slow exactly, and not hard gazers, but God told me this car was coming around a second time. I jumped, made the announcement, and frenzy ensued for a thorough straightening. Sure enough, they came around again and wished to set a viewing appointment. The very reason for the flexibility is to not lose them when you have them. So, we invited a lady, with her mother, in to present the entire place. She loved it! Well, so did everyone else that viewed the house and we never heard from them again. Upon visiting afterward, we learned she had previously found our house on *Craiglist*, and then saw the post office sign.

Springtime 2010 saw our baby, Josiah, born and the house price increase from $120,000 to $130,000, but an economic recession forced us to lower it to $110,000 that summer. This provided just enough to pay off the remaining loan. As there were numerous foreclosures and auctions in our area, we were informed several times that our house would not sell. Nevertheless, we hung our newly printed posters in the post office on Monday, August 9th. The following day, Tuesday, a black truck pulled up. By the time the family unloaded, we were ready. It turned out our lady had persuaded her husband to view it himself. Our first second-viewing! I met them outside to walk them around before entering the house. Very quickly it was established they came due to the new post office sign, and, without a realtor! Yay! However, they left without portraying visual interest or emotion, and a lack of commitment. So, the week continued. Sunday August 15th, the husband telephoned. He anxiously explained they had their loan papers ready to turn in Monday and had called to verbally commit to purchasing, as-is condition, for the full asking price. The following day, Tuesday, he again called to confirm the paperwork was in and proceeded to ask if he could come and sign the contract that same afternoon. All of a sudden our house was sold and we needed to move out by October 1st!

We never worried about where we would go after we sold, as God would show us when it was time. It turned out a gentleman we view as our uncle owned a vacated house right here in Mullan. In fact, he was planning on someday running it to the ground. When we approached him concerning this subject, it was agreed that if we would make it livable, and then continue to fix it up little by little, we could live there rent free. Luke began his work. God paved the way by providing a toilet with new guts, bathroom vanity and sink, a great washer and dryer set, and futon couch and mattress (which was to be our bed for quite awhile). All of it was for free, except the futon which cost us twenty dollars!

Two weeks before we were to move out, a man addressed Luke. He invited us to his church. That Sunday we shared worship and dinner with Christian Mennonites for the first time. During the next week, this man's father stopped by to visit. He expressed his desire to aid Luke in any area of our new house. Luke, noting the genuine sincerity of his guest, replied plumbing was his largest need.

God really pressed urgency upon our blessed helper. I was prepared for no kitchen cupboards or counter, and no water. Thankfully, our ever-caring Father thought we needed more. Instead, our move-in day had cold running water to the bathroom tub, toilet, and sink. Hooray! Hallelujah! The next day God brought His helper back to finish servicing the hot water lines. He found the tank needed replaced. Asking Luke's permission to install a new one, and Luke consenting that he could and would pay him in return, our gentleman stated he had already picked one up on that day. Consequently, he began the replacement process and I gathered cash. Luke arrived home as our helper finished. When he was preparing to leave, Luke inquired what he owed (it was always circumvented before). The returned answer was, "nothing." Luke pressed that we were fully able and wanted to pay, but he would accept nothing for supplies or labor. We tried to at least compensate him for the hot water tank, and he finally turned and humbly declared, "God knows how to bless me," and that was enough. Luke was very touched at this gentleman's example of faith and loving trust in God.

We can thank God for His love, which surpasses our understanding, because without it, we wouldn't have these stories to tell. Once we receive God's love within us, it first being given to us and exemplified for us, hearts like this man's, or others', could never be. If our beloved God loves us enough to send His Son to die for us before we even acknowledge His Son's name, before we have any relationship, while we are yet steeped in fleshly pleasures and lusts, simply because He created us, how much more abundantly will His caresses, watchfulness, provisions, love, and discipline be granted for His *faithful* children. Not for perfection sake, but for faith in His Son and Himself.

What matters most in life is where our faith is. Even with the final tribulations, whether God makes one invisible in the city or the mountains, raises us up as martyrs, feeds by heavenly manna or by diligently prepared storage, we must focus on the powerful truth that God is in control. We need to have the desire to live or die as He sees fit, for His glory. These coming times are not for the nonbelievers only; it will also prove all who claim Jesus as their Lord. Why fear anything that was set forth by God? No matter what, our Divine Deliverer has a perfect plan and we need to trust that. May we all be willing and ready individuals for anything God has intended. May we all trust only in His Son Jesus Christ, who is Lord of Salvation, with the hope of eternal life in Him.

CHAPTER 18

The Story of Brayden

Once upon a time, there was a baby boy named Brayden. As an infant, he was taken into the loving arms of his grandmother who sacrificed her own pleasures to care of this precious boy. A little after Brayden's first birthday, in November 2009, his grandma approached a family with five young children, and asked them outright to adopt this little boy. She saw his need for a loving family, children to play with, and parents to train him. She loved her grandson very much but recognized she, as a widow, would have great difficulty in fulfilling the role of mother, father, grandma, grandpa, provider, disciplinarian, and nurturer, all at the same time.

This family she went to saw the Bible as the most treasured love letter ever written. It held very valuable instructions, warnings, and promises which have never failed them to be the right course in every aspect of life; proving itself to be the only Book of truth, time and time again. In it can be found the gift God offers to everyone. This gift, as you know, is Jesus, God's only begotten Son. Jesus humbly submitted to freely undertake the responsibility for our sins so we might someday live forever with His—and our—loving Father God. This family enjoyed the merciful and gracious opportunities to begin anew, through Christ their Savior, every time they disobeyed God's written Word. Due to the tender discipline, love, and encouragement from God's close relationship, this family was extremely thankful and thus strove to do everything in their feeble power to live in obedience to His Will. They hoped their returned love would be pleasing to Him.

This family of seven was not perfect at all. God is their true witness to how often they all fell short, but the blood and body of our Savior would again cover their sins in forgiveness when they repented. How thankful and rejoiceful that family is for this ultimate blessing. They also submitted their lives to enjoy *God's* rewards instead of those offered by the world. This was not always easy for them, as their selfishness would covet convenience and their own pleasures many times, but our patient God was very tender in His mercies toward this growing family and allowed them to see through His eyes several times, which opened new faith and understanding into His vision. An example is found in Matthew 19 as Jesus rebukes his disciples who don't want the children because they view them as inconvenient or in the way. Jesus corrects the model when he follows-up the rebuke by saying "Suffer little children, and forbid them not to come to me: for of such is the kingdom of heaven." "And [Jesus] took a little child, and set him in the midst of them, and took him in his arms, and said unto them, Whosoever shall receive one of such little children in my Name, receiveth me: and whosoever receiveth me, receiveth not me, but him that sent me" (Mark 9:36-37). God had taught this little family many lessons and performed numerous miracles as He showed Himself to them, and they tried their best to glorify Him in return.

The wife had at one point pondered in her thoughts with the Lord if He would ever want them to adopt. Following this contemplation, she communed that it would have to be a miracle as they did not have finances to do such a thing, but she gave credit to her Lord saying she knew He was the holder of all riches and He could also bring about such *impossible* occurrences quite easily. The pondering was left there.

When the aforementioned grandmother sought out this young family, asking them to take this little boy into their family, adopting him as one of their own, it was received with much humility. Who can stand under such honor from our Lord, for this family was much aware of their shortcomings. However, they were also aware of their sweet Lord's sovereignty over every situation. It was with peace they agreed to help her and the little boy as much as they could.

However, soon the course changed. The grandmother needed to attain guardianship instead, and the little family became babysitters for Brayden. This was quite a turn for the family, but they always took great comfort knowing that God knew what was best for them, the grandmother, and Brayden. So, they took care of him only occasionally. Eventually the need arose for weekly care. The wife enjoyed this process with quiet wonderings if the Lord were actually weaning their family into this new adoptive role. But, those wonderings were merely kept in the hearts of those parents with a smile and trust to their God. Time progressed to move from nightly watches to night and all morning before grandma would pick her grandson up for dinner and return that night for a second day repeated. Weeks went by and God stamped this little boy and his grandmother on the hearts of every member in the family.

As the 2010 year ended and the family returned home from a vacation, they brought back with them a plan, a plan to renew

the adoption procedure. All week previously, they had sought
wisdom and prayer concerning Braden. Adoption had never been
mentioned since the initial encounter. Well, the spoken-of family
wished to open up their lives to receive unto themselves a new
son and grandmother, *if*, and only if it were God's will. Prayers
were lifted up for the grandmother's heart to be prepared and for
themselves to be submissive to whichever result God thought best.
They knew their wonderful Father in Heaven would only give them
what they and He could handle together.

By the time the appointed evening arrived, this young husband
and wife had gone through many doubts regarding their ability to
give this little boy what he needed, doubts on whether they could
properly train up his soul to love God, and doubts because they
knew how often they messed up. Then reality followed with how
the Lord was working with their children up to this time. Although
their portrait on parenting was not top-notch, they tried in Jesus'
name, and continually prayed for God to make those scribbles
into a work of art for His own glory. God was creating results that
blessed those parents tremendously. Hours before the arrival of the
pair, the wife asked her beloved Lord if He could possibly stand
such a thing as to have them lean on Him that much more! The
strength needed to give this boy what he needed, the patience and
wisdom to care for him and his grandmother, the duties attached
to the circumstances, etc, seemed too much. And it was too much
for them. But it wasn't too much for their God who specializes in
the impossible.

That night, the parents of this family, Brayden, and his grandma
sat together in conversation those several minutes before Grandma's
departure. The husband of this family had decided they might be
rushing into this talk and informed his wife to not say anything
that night. But God directed the conversation in such a manner

that the husband later said he felt the push and peace to begin their inquiry. So, gently, he made his request on behalf of the whole family. Immediately, reply came back with an excited "Yes, I've been thinking the same thing and didn't know when to mention it!"

God is so great! The handwriting was on the wall! It is such a wonderful feeling to know you are in God's Will. And the immense security knowing God will see His plan through with the necessary provisions, the granting of increased love and wisdom we need, is beyond words. God will never leave us nor forsake us.

As you have probably guessed, this family is ours. My darling husband, my five children, and I have received the blessing of another son. And, we have received the blessing of another mother and grandmother. When we first asked the children of their opinion in the matter, they loudly and joyously exclaimed "YEAH! We will have another brother to play with! YEAH! YEAH!" We are very excited, greatly humbled, and honored to be trusted with the precious souls of Brayden Woods and his grandmother. As we integrate Brayden into being a full time Munsen, I realize he is precisely the miracle I pondered on just a short time ago.

Never underestimate the power of God. If you find something impossible, joyfully give it to God and watch Him work it out in the best possible manner. And you will learn that it is in your best interest to submit everything in your life, big and small, to His most perfect capable hands as well. Brayden turned two years old the end of November, 2010.

I regret to inform you of a bittersweet update. After only two official months with our new son (end of January 2011), Grandma came to take Brayden home. She declared she missed him terribly and felt like she abandoned her grandson. She had invested so much time and effort for his sake that it simply didn't seem right to leave him now. Her home was not the same without him. In the end, she confessed that it was best for Brayden to stay with us, but *she* needed *him*. We wept, as our hearts had quite taken him in already. However, I believe our part was finished. Where Grandma had waivered before, wondering what to do, she was now firmly decided to hold on to and raise her grandson as her own. This decision was important for the both of them.

Honestly, there were some demanding times through this transition, but we were and are blessed to have had this chapter in our life. Brayden will always be remembered.

CHAPTER 19

Wanted: A Willing Vessel for my Service

The prospect of weaning Josiah around a year of age brought with it a crossroad decision. A highly controversial one as well, and one that tested our faith...

In the first chapter of Genesis, we find the first instructions for mankind: "And God blessed them, and God said unto them, Be fruitful and multiply, and replenish the earth, and subdue it: and have dominion over the fish of the sea, and over the fowl of the air, and over every living thing that moveth upon the earth" (Genesis 1:28). It wasn't long before mankind became exceedingly wicked. Consequently, God planned to destroy all humans, but had mercy on Noah and his family. We see the human creation continued through eight people due to a faithful patriarch who was obedient, just, and righteous. Immediately following the exit of the ark, after the flood, "God blessed Noah and his sons, and said unto them, Be fruitful and multiply and replenish the earth" (Genesis 9:1). During God's speech, it was only six verses later we hear, "And you, be ye fruitful, and multiply, bring forth *abundantly* in the earth, and multiply therein" (Genesis 9:7). If any held confusion about the word "replenish" in the former verse, it was cleared up in the repeat of the same command. Replenish means to "fill, make plenty," but sounds like it is conditional to our culture and views of population. The follow-up clarifies God wants abundance and to multiply without end. He loves how the math works out. Just think, if Christians all have ten kids, those kids have ten kids, who have ten kids, we have an army for God in three generations. One faithful couple would be the start of one-thousand souls to serve our Lord in merely three generations. Multiply that by all married Christians. Is this why our Creator, our God, mandated this?

Well, anyway, we cannot find one single verse that has ended this directive. On the contrary, we have several that support and encourage this very command. Some well known ones are Psalm 127 and Psalm 128. God actually calls children His inheritance and His reward to us! Wait, there's more! The man that fears the Lord and walks in His ways will be blessed by eating "the labor of (his) hands" and "happy shalt thou be, and it shall be well with thee. Thy wife shall be as a fruitful vine…thy children like olive plants round about thy table. Behold, thus shall the man be blessed that feareth the Lord." What an incredible vision!

Did you ever wonder why God designed man and woman to need one another so much? I enjoy dwelling on the pure intelligence of our design. It is absolutely amazing! It's simply beyond my ability to comprehend it all. Nevertheless, I do feel the very instinct that drives a man and woman to desire being one flesh physically is to fulfill God's purposed original commandment. This drive, held under control until holy matrimony between one man and one woman only, God declares is acceptable to all and the bed undefiled (Hebrew 13:4). God has provided the instinctive motivation to fulfill his intent that we be fruitful, and multiply our numbers. The design fits the command!

In the wonderful book of Malachi, the scriptures reveal why God ordained and created one wife for a husband. It reads, "And did not he make one...And wherefore one? That He might seek a godly seed. Therefore take heed to your spirit, and let none deal treacherously against the wife of his youth" (Malachi 2:15). If our Creator made marriage because He seeks a godly seed, then so should we.

We have felt the strains of parenting. Most of those strains are a direct result of selfishness. Inconvenience when our children need help or messes are made; exasperation at the constant attention required to properly train, designate tasks and follow-up supervision, guiding thoughts, remarks, behavior, and emotions; and sinful irritation at the noise of questions, laughter, playing, and crying (and sometimes all at the same time) have left me frazzled by the day's end. It feels similar to a spinning whirlwind and having nothing visually accomplished to show for it, at least not in our exhausted eyes. Satan has often seized these moments where we should instead feel privileged for having been trusted to care for these precious charges. We should feel hope that our attentiveness would please our gracious Father. We should feel as if we've participated in the most important ministry of all...tending to the hearts and souls of *God's* children. Why not feel as though we have accomplished the most on these days (providing proper discipline is not the problem). After all, it's these very duties that shape our children, whom we will carry to eternity with us.

Upon weaning Josiah, we wanted to "take a break" from more children for a few years. As I began recording my early morning temperature to note my ovulation and fertile days, I was worried someone would ask me if I was planning another baby. I felt convicted and ashamed at having to answer. Discussing this with Luke, we learned the shameful feelings resulted from faithless decisions and actions. Why would we usurp God's authority to take matters into our own hands? One, we thought my body needed a break. Two, we were not stopping, just creating space between one batch and the next. Three, we were *scared*. Scared of more responsibility, and scared because we felt inadequate. Four, the thoughts of freedom and indulgences were tempting us.

These four selfish reasons caused us to lay aside scripture and deny God's blessings and inheritance. Through these four compromising excuses, we rationalized disobeying our Creator's wishes and vision. How terribly faithless! We *should* be ashamed to put our thoughts and plans above God's. There is a question that we have heard only when equipping for a rationalized excuse. It goes like this: "Yah, but God gave us a brain to use, too!" To us, the response to this question is, "do we submit one-hundred percent of ourselves to God, or do we part it out?" We wish to use our brain, to the best of our earthly ability, to enjoy following biblical scripture, and to love God's vision.

We have declared to commit our lives and souls to our loving God through our Lord and Savior Jesus Christ. If, therefore, we say we have given our bodies and lives over to God, then that includes our *entire* body. This implies one-hundred percent, not everything but the uterus, or the eyes, or the stomach, etc.

We often hear how our Sovereign God has closed the womb of women, sometimes after one, or several, children. Sometimes for five to eight years before their womb was opened (by Divine intervention only and not through a fertility program). Sometimes the closing occurred between children, and sometimes in its entirety. Therefore, we feel we shouldn't need to play God and create space when *we* want it. Thankfully, even imperfect bodies are under our Master Designer's hands. For me, when I die, whenever that is, I want to be performing God's Will.

We were definitely being challenged about faith. Did we truly believe God could and *would* control my womb? Did we believe He could provide for every life He created? Did we honestly trust Him for *every* area of our lives? Did we really want to submit ourselves to be joyful vessels for *whatever* God has planned? Interestingly, for three fertile months during this uncertain period of prayer and study, we received the visual aid of God's manipulation. Every month of indecision, God's mercy and patience providentially caused ovulation to start the first day of menses, thus, no pregnancies.

I believe "being fruitful and multiplying" is still part of God's design and will for women, hence for me. It does not mean I will never be tempted by fear. It does mean we have *One* who is more capable than ourselves. *One* who will help us carry forth, with Him, the great design of bringing forth and nurturing life. What about the future? That will take care of itself and we will still be learning then, too. I have never been in every situation possible for every woman, so please do not feel condemned because we feel this way for our circumstance. We cannot judge for you. Just be encouraged to seek God for His wisdom to help you sift out all your motivations. It is between you and Him, and He will know what is deep within your heart. So do not worry what men think. We also feel it's important to try to stay blameless as examples of godly Christians to the world. Consequently, it was with a clear conscious we submitted our uterus to God as a vessel for His created life should He want to use it.

We are happy to announce that we became pregnant the following month, in April 2011. God willing, this gifted blessing will be born the end of January 2012.

CHAPTER 20

Titus Robert Munsen

~ Born February 2, 2012 ~

I love how God can use any situation to bring about good change. When this pregnancy—my sixth—began, my first reaction was excitement upon learning of the new little life. My second reaction came several days later: I was truly shocked! I had completely believed we wouldn't be conceiving anymore. When we renewed ourselves to God's Will, I felt we stood vulnerable and exposed before His throne. Surely He knew every sin, every unloving, wrong thing we've ever enacted to our children. He definitely would not trust us with any more! I was wrong. For some reason, He wanted us to love and train up another child with Him. Moving past the surprise, we found comfort that God trusted us to improve and do better. Wanting deeply to do it right and please Him in this important area of stewardship, we *are* very thankful we don't have to do it alone. We always have our Heavenly Father and Counselor to seek for strength, wisdom, help, and hope.

Following this consolation came another foreboding feeling, as though a guilty secret was yet undiscovered. It would often cause me to sadly weep, but I did not know why. I searched every plausible reason. All I could do was cry out from my soul to God. All I knew to cry out was "Help! Please, Lord, help me!"

One day, we were visiting friends and the topic of confessing our weaknesses to others began. That conversation was the instrument which finally cleared my confusion. God revealed to me the cause of my foreboding sadness: anger in my tones. I did not wish to display it to yet another child. I already couldn't completely control my impatience with the children I currently had. It was not constant, but it did happen. This was the sin I thought God had missed. Guiltiness was convicting my soul. How could He want another child under my ungodly influence? As much as I desired it, I failed to conquer my evil flesh. It seemed God had overlooked a big iniquity in my life, and if He knew, then surely I couldn't be trusted.

Therefore, when the "secret" came under scrutiny the relief from confession began breaking my bondage. I feared another child because I feared my children would be like me and then have a lack of control and not gain authority over their anger. I was too ashamed of my behavior to honestly ask God for help in the correct degree that was necessary. However, I could not hide anymore. It was all in the open. My hideous sins were known. My Lord helped me realize it's not I who can "conquer" me, it's He. I am simply supposed to surrender all, and believe He has died for them, making me new. Luke and I rejoiced exceedingly as we both went before the throne. The freedom of released burdens and guilt, then of the forgiveness and renewal, was powerful.

Galatians 5:19-20 lists ungodly lusts. In this passage, my spotlighted sin appeared: "Now the works of the flesh are manifest, which are these: adultery, fornication, uncleanness, lasciviousness, idolatry, witchcraft, hatred, variance, emulations, *wrath*, strife, seditions, heresies, envyings, murders, drunkenness, revelries, and such like: of the which I tell you before, as I have also told you in the past, that they which do such things shall not inherit the kingdom of God."

Colossians 3:8 instructs us to put aside anger. "But now ye also put off all these: anger, wrath, malice, blasphemy, filthy communication out of your mouth." The Bible doesn't teach in degrees, so it is entirely irrelevant to separate irritation from rage. It is *all* anger and we are to put it away from us.

After Jesus gracefully expelled our demons, we implored the space to be filled with our Master's love so we could in turn learn to love our children better. Jesus Christ's blood and body could take authority over my sins, where my own might failed. Although I no longer needed exasperation to give me "an edge" in bringing about order in the family, we did need to set guard against the old temptation. We both made a pact to change. Praising our wonderful counselor and God, I now looked ahead with excitement. I was also very humbled that God really knew and hadn't given up. As long as we seek Him for help and guidance, then perhaps we can honor His name after all, and someday return His created souls back to Him!

Before this pregnancy I was taking my base temperature each morning. This gave me the blessing of watching it rise and remain steady at least half a degree or more, visually showing pregnancy. We never even took a pregnancy test! Two weeks along, it settled with assurance that God had blessed us with a boy. Of course, I could not know for sure, but it just felt so clear. Luke joyfully picked out the name Titus for his earthly life, with

Robert as his middle name. This carries from Luke's stepfather, Robert Chitwood, or Grandpa Bob. We never did pick out a definite girl's name. We figured to wait and decide after the birth if it was a girl.

That summer found lots of busy preparations. We had moved into a house that needed everything fixed up. Upon learning of our pregnancy, we desired to finish our bedrooms so we could function easier with a new baby. God granted this request and provided the resources to complete all the bedrooms in the house. Before this, all the kids shared the master bedroom, and we had the living room futon (for a year and a-half almost). Not impossible, but not ideal for childbirth, recovery, a new baby, or normal living. God even provided another $250 through the bank again! Just like before, this money miraculously emerged out of nowhere! Consulting the bank, we all went through our records, and their systems, saw the total was not amiss, and the funds were true. What heavenly provisions! Luke confessed he had believed the first time to be my error and doubted the miracle, but he now saw God in them both.

Around thirteen weeks, I bled a little for several days, accompanied by light belly hugs but without cramps. We gave the baby to God's healing and care and rested a lot. At twenty-nine weeks, my contractions lightly began again. I was concerned my body was doomed to not carry full term anymore. God used water, rest, wild yam salve, and prayer to help us through. Besides these two occurrences, we were blessed with an incredibly healthy pregnancy. I diligently consumed prenatal vitamins in addition to my herbal teas of mostly red raspberry, then alfalfa, nettle, and dandelion. Second trimester added squawvine, peppermint, and black haw root (cramp bark) to the mix, and thirty-seven weeks added black cohosh. We remembered to practice the Bradley

Method exercises at thirty-two weeks. I was carrying well, slept well, and continued to feel strong, active, and energetic. I had nothing to complain about.

Luke was excited to participate more intimately in this birth, and requested to be solo with me. This was a great plan to me. So, Luke tentatively arranged for Grandma to take the kids for several days. And, he not only encouraged my exercise activities, he created time for me to accomplish them, as well as to perform them with me!

We had a guest arriving at forty-one and a-half weeks, Tuesday, and confidence was felt that no baby would come as long as we had company. It would be too much for me when sleepless nights and nursing began. God won't give us more than we can handle. As our guest would stay until Friday or Saturday, we happily settled in for a February baby. Well, February 1st, Wednesday, was an encouraging day as I had strong contractions all day and into the night. I welcomed each one as I hoped it meant much less during labor. Strangely, Bill, our guest, received a phone call which summoned him away first thing Thursday morning. I couldn't help but wonder if God was orchestrating all the details of the event because He planned on us having our baby soon. Anyhow, Bill retired Wednesday night at 9:30 pm, and I was still pregnant. Luke and I went straight to bed.

At 10:24 pm I awoke due to a *different* contraction and amazed that we would finally see our baby boy or girl that next day. Focusing on relaxing and not getting excited, I managed to sleep until 12:30 am. At this point, I couldn't relax efficiently as pool and birth preparations loomed in my mind. Therefore, I woke Luke and he began his work. I remained in bed another half hour conversing with my Great Physician, my comforting Father in Heaven. Around 2:00 am, all was ready.

I planned to sleep and rest in my "hot tub" with the soft music and candlelight while labor progressed. However, there was no time for naps, as progression continued in leaps and bounds. Earlier, upon cleaning the floor on my hands and knees, during a contraction, I discovered the pangs would move off my stomach and locate as back labor. It seemed so much *easier*. Using this new knowledge, I wasn't aware that the contractions had become very close together. Luke had noticed, but I'm glad he never told me. Everything seemed so much more bearable with the back labor that I still figured we had several hours before hard labor began. Perhaps I was heavily concentrating on the moment.

With this mindset, the next contraction shocked me. There seemed to be no warning, just "BAM!" I was completely caught off guard. The new intensity, the need to push, the pressure, etc. sent me from peaceful relaxation to sharp awareness. I expressed aloud to God that "I wasn't ready for that; it was too much too fast. I need a moment to collect!" Mercifully, I had that moment, and more, to think.

Now, following that one contraction, transition was over and full understanding of where we were in the birth was realized. I proceeded to "moo" through the next pangs. It all seemed so new and different! It was then I felt the water bag break, which preceded the immediate delivery.

In an instant, energy swept over me and the hard work was over. I informed Luke our baby was indeed a boy and upon surfacing his head, I noticed the cord draped like a scarf over his shoulders. Our Titus was not breathing on his own, but through the umbilical cord. We praised God for the long cord that was easily slipped off. Titus had great color and his hands and feet had movement. Upon some tender loving care, he coughed. Then he cried a lusty cry to match his husky frame and chubby cheeks.

Soon, he settled and began experimenting with movements in the water. First, he extended one limb and quickly retracted it to extend another until he had confidence and comfort enough to relax all. It was a lot of fun to watch him!

Titus was born at 3:10 am on February 2, 2012, making labor nearly five hours. The afterbirth delivered completely whole, proving another prayer granted. Bleeding was minimal, labor and birth all at night, and I had Luke all to myself! Every request granted, every detail taken care of. God carried us through the entire labor! Luke was very wonderful as well. From quitting his sleep readily to get the pool all set and the shower cleaned, to actively answering my every need, which was to keep touch contact and to talk to me. We both knew everything we spoke was heard by our attentive Father in Heaven as well as immediately answered. I felt carried on a sea of miracles!

Luke says he never saw me trust God so much as there was no sense of panic throughout the entire labor. The only time he was worried was when it took a few minutes for Titus to breathe, but was comforted upon declaring him God's. After Titus cried, we heard the children jump and run to the stairs where they remained respectfully waiting for us to come to them. Luke had fun answering their inquiries of "boy or girl?"

My baby and I are completely healthy. God proved He could bring me through prenatal, pregnancy, birth, and delivery, strong and capable. He showed us He could use my body to carry a stout baby, well past the "due date." Having another large baby was a concern Luke held for me, but God demonstrated He would combat even that fear for him. God has shown through our healthy birth and recovery, that He can carry it all. It is great personal satisfaction to me that Titus was not born until February (my due date was January 20th) and that he was the size he was. God is undeniably in control! The whole journey from pre-pregnancy through birth was an enriching experience. Why must we fear anything when our magnificent Creator wants to be so intimately involved? Thank you! Thank you, Beloved Savior, that we can have open the avenue to such a loving God!

That morning, our friend Bill never even suspected the surprise we had waiting for him! You can imagine the shock when he arrived early to say goodbye and we carried out a brand new baby! I will never forget that morning! After we welcomed and invited him to share breakfast with us, we asked him if he would like to see our new baby. In disbelief he looked at my abdomen, and relief flooded his face when he saw that I wasn't skinny yet. He laughed at our good joke, but as Luke disappeared into the bedroom, his eyes began to grow in realization that it wasn't a joke after all. He was the first to meet Titus, at only five hours old. For a man who is never short on words, he ate a silent breakfast with us that morning!

Later that morning, Luke wrapped up our newest gift, and took him down the street to weigh him. There, our Titus weighed in at 9 pounds, 9 ½ ounces. Luke had correctly guessed his weight between nine and ten pounds. At home, he measured 22 inches long, with a head circumference of 14 ¼ inches. We feel extremely blessed and thankful to be allowed by our Heavenly Father to birth this way, very thankful indeed! Praises and glory to God!

Luke and I both want to extend a word of note to mothers and fathers: We firmly believe in a ten-day minimal recovery period where the mother does not leave her bedroom but for bathroom/ shower breaks (perhaps infrequent rocking chair time with the family). We didn't have this to start with but have learned it the hard way. There in her room, the mother may establish nursing or feeding, bond with her baby, sleep, read or write, and just have some quiet peace and rest while her physical body is healing, and emotions are adjusting.

Fathers, in this way, you are gifting a great start toward her new phase of motherhood, especially if there are children already. Consequently, it is up to *you* to schedule, become, or allow her to schedule, a helper fit to care and cook, a safe influence, and a proper disciplinarian for the children. That person must be a proper disciplinarian so the mother will not have the double work of getting them back to normal after the helper is gone. This way she really is comfortable to relax the "radar" and recover. Even if she feels great and capable, this period should be there for long-term health and out of respect to what her body just went through. Or, husbands, if you can do this yourself, then take the time to give your whole attention to this matter, tenderly and sympathetically caring for her (it will be a great time to dote love notes on her as well)! Allow the children to partake in bringing her meals in bed; they will love to show this love and service and think it great fun! It also gives them the reward of doing-for-others (and to see the new baby). Encourage them to write or color love notes to set upon her plate, this creates more bonding between mother and children as well. Mother should greet them with lots of words of praise and adoration for their help and nurturing care toward her. I believe this goes along way in preventing depression and burn out.

I share this especially, because this recovery was not there following this birth. My time seemed to be disordered as I disappeared in snatches to nurse or lay upon my bed amongst the noise on the other side of the wall, not able to sleep. Without this encouragement or order to rest from my husband, I felt much too selfish to do so myself as I did feel great, at first, except for the tiredness and painful nursing.

Husbands, you may need to be firm and active in this recovery plan so she really believes this *is indeed* what you want and there is no sense of any crossed wires. This time, I was not sure where I belonged. I heard his words that I could rest if I wanted to, but the goings-on outside the bedroom showed me he seemed to be too overwhelmed, so I couldn't rest. I needed to help *him*.

The meals that were brought to us helped tremendously, as neither Luke nor I had to worry about cooking. Once everyone was sitting down and eating, I could sneak in a nap. It was only like this for a few weeks. Then, after more frequent episodes of crying out for help on my part, Luke finally decided it was important that he try to not use his home time to work on the house and began structuring and guiding the children. However, I think it was too late, and for the first time, I was absolutely burnt out and scared I was headed for a complete melt-down, whatever that was. I was so behind on sleep and rest, so exhausted from crying, my head constantly hurt, and my mind was clouded. I couldn't keep anything straight or organized, and everything seemed a chore. I only lasted a few hours each day with activity, and I continued to head downhill. My emotions constantly kept my hormones in a state of upheaval. The devil was telling me lies against my husband, and using this time to create marital difficulties. Yet, God didn't allow me to be tricked with these, as He kept me completely aware of where those thoughts were coming from. However, I couldn't seem to make the right choices. I could no longer feel any love, and the constant prayer was again, "HELP! I NEED HELP!"

Luke was extremely patient with me. He was a quick forgiver and learner with my bitterness toward him. He would still somehow choose to love me and give me hugs to help me through, even when

I was so low I could never respond to any of these offerings. With a lack of love, I became sensitive, but to combat arguments arising, I became silent because I didn't trust my feelings and tongue. Luke saw this as my giving up and putting up a wall between us, so he would talk it over until I gave vent to my thoughts, and this brought self-loathing and guilt that I failed again at not guarding my annoyances. On the other hand, it did force me to open myself back up to him.

I didn't know how God was going to help me. Where Luke missed my needs, God afterward used him as my vessel for healing. I am so thankful He did. Little by little, when my burdens were eased, and I only had to school from late morning to noon, sleep, eat, and read my Bible with more routine and understanding, I felt peace come. At that time, I could focus on God and choose to love my husband again. A hair cut eased the head ache symptoms as well. Rather than feeling generally recovered and refreshed two weeks following childbirth, it took two and a-half months. It's always easier to do it right the first time. The victory came when I laid down my flesh and asked Christ and His love to reign in my heart. God had to be my fulfillment—not my husband.

I began sharing this with other women and found out that most mothers seemed to have moments of being burnt out and some even experienced "nervous breakdowns" or melt-downs. The general feeling and knowledge of these burn-outs were due to a lack of nutrition and vitamins. They were not being negligent about their own choices and actions. It just couldn't be ignored that taking a good daily vitamin with minerals really helped them not feel fatigued. Let's face it. Our bodies get depleted during pregnancy and nursing, it makes sense to need to replete them. So, the advice is: lots of God's Word, a quiet recovery period, good vitamins, and lots of water.

CHAPTER 21

A Note on Child Training

I'm sure you've heard the saying "children don't come with an instruction manual". Well, there is one! We just have to pull it out and use it. This manual is the Bible. We simply cannot expound or write anything more helpful or encouraging than what is already provided for all. We only need to trust and obey. Who can know any better than He, who is our Master Creator? Only He can know the best way to train us up.

The above is enough and should be enough for this chapter because no ONE family can find the ONE way for all other families to train up their children. It's by God's Word, grace, and love, only through His Son's blood, that any of us and any of our children live a life of victory. It's not because we as parents are good, it's not because we as parents are Bible scholars. And, as much as the world thinks so, it certainly is not because our children are born "good." It's by prayer, a thankful heart, rejoicing love, patience, and taking them with you as a family to lay down your lives to serve God's people. However, many have asked for us to record some of our thoughts due to the blessings our six children have provided them.

Please understand that we all are different and God has given each of us our children because he knows who we are and what children need what parents.

Rather than thinking from the evolutionist stages of development, let us imagine only two phases of life: Old Testament and New Testament. The Old Testament exemplifies cause and effect: command, disobedience, and discipline; or command, obedience, and blessings. The general theme of training is systematic, consistent, and eye for an eye. Rules are taught, established, and expected. Envision our babies to about five or eight years of age in the Old Testament. These characters obey from fear—or trust—of the Lord's consistent judgment and discipline, and faith that the words spoken are true.

Next, we hold the New Testament. Once the age of understanding arrives, then we transition into the New Testament. At this point, we learn to incorporate more grace, mercy, love, and patience. These are also integrated in the Old Testament, but take the front seat during the New Testament. No longer does "eye for an eye" take effect. Individuals in this last stage of life further their understanding by cultivations of tender patience, longsuffering, love, and comfort as well as chastisement, rebukes, and corrections.

If we look for examples in the Bible, we have two young men to consider. Remember Hannah's son, Samuel? When God called this young sleeper, Samuel promptly jumped out of bed and *ran* to the priest. He was alert, aware, and ready; not lazy, but obedient. He then appropriately and respectfully addressed his elder. When told to return to bed, he showed responsibility to do so capably and completely on his own. Then, called from his sleep a second time, he immediately obeyed the summons, inquired respectfully, and retired again. The third time, he still demonstrated these character qualities. When sleep was disturbed, he proved his well-trained clean heart by the unfailing, unhesitating actions time and time again. If he had any "self" ruling, he would have grumbled about being awakened and groaned when he actually had to get out of bed. The third repetition would not have been equally respectful or as prompt.

Another example we can draw from exemplifies a twelve-year-old. This young man shows us a new landmark. By that age our children should be completely competent, trustworthy, obedient, responsible, respectful, and God-minded. Have you guessed who our example is? He entirely took care of himself for three days: fed himself, bought for himself, found lodging for himself, chose appropriate associations for himself, spoke respectfully and appropriately, and spent his time learning of God's word. Even after displaying this, he submissively obeyed the summons of his parents. Have you guessed Jesus? Then you are correct! It is our beloved Savior who shows us what to expect from a twelve-year-old.

Deuteronomy, chapter six, lays out the blueprint of parenting: "Thou shalt love the Lord thy God with all thine heart, and with all thy soul, and with all thy might. And these words, which I command thee this day, shall be in thine heart..." Let's pause there. You first have to be what you want your children to be. You guide, teach, and lead them as God guides, teaches, and leads you (and at the same time), "...and thou shalt teach them *diligently* unto thy children, and shalt talk of them when thou sittest in thine house, and when thou walkest by the way, and when thou liest down, and when thou risest up. And thou shalt bind them for a sign upon thine hand, and they shall be as frontlets between thine eyes. And thou shalt write them upon the posts of thy house, and on thy gates." I don't know about you but we seem to always be in the middle of one of these situations. Thus, it just doesn't leave any time to be away from the children, even for schooling. Instead, it sets forth the parents as preferred teachers.

"WAIT!" you say? "I don't have any experience! I don't know how to teach! I'm not that smart!" Well, then you make the best ingredient for a recipe of success. This will cause you to pray and depend upon God for everything. And God loves to perform for those who trust in Him. "My grace is sufficient for thee, for my strength is made perfect in weakness…" (2Corinthians 12:9-11). We can say this from personal experience. Neither one of us were homeschooled, and yet we are granted perfect ability and insight to perform this grand role every day. On a deeper and more personal note, none of us knows how much longer we will be together on this earth. Some have experienced a fullness of the home school blessing that we have not, when they have lost their children.

Before we go on, I want to express the importance of love. No method of training will work without it. Tie strings of love with your children by enjoying the things they like. Genuinely smile at them, it will surprise you what this simple act can do. Eat your meals with them. It's also very important for parents to search ways to praise good character qualities. However, you will be your own enemy if you praise vain things, thus building up "pride" and "self". By these I mean, "you're so smart!", or "you're so pretty!" In the third appendix, you will find a list of character qualities. Find out what these mean and use them instead. Your children will benefit greatly when you praise their "attentiveness" when learning and their "diligence" to finish their work. This doubles by adding to their vocabulary lessons as well. Search ways to praise the good ten times more than you need to correct them. This will save you from having so many corrections and allows you to lead them into good behavior habits with love and fun. Also, we find that when the children are feeling useful and fulfilled as needed members of the family they naturally behave with maturity.

Assuming a healthy relationship exists, let's continue to Ephesians 6:4, "Fathers, provoke not your children to anger, but bring them up in the nurture and admonition of the Lord." Also Colossians 3:21 reads, "Fathers, provoke not your children to anger, lest they be discouraged." Bitterness is a seed that will steal your child's heart. Fast, constant, and consistent training will not confuse. Remember anger begets anger. It, along with high emotions, are poison to a child.

I find it quite wonderful that children do not remember much in the first five years of life. Wonderful because it's these years that most training *should* be accomplished. When discipline is the result of fair judgment, they don't recall the incident. On the contrary, when emotions run high (or tempers), or when we react instead of consider, then the memory remains. Our children testify of this very thing. So God's first help to us is to offer the blessing of erasing any memories of proper discipline and punishment, while holding the lessons given.

The instruction manual names the tool best used for training: the rod. It also names the placement as "the back of him" as in Proverbs 10:13: "in the lips of him that has understanding wisdom is found, but the rod is for the back of him that is void of understanding." Those who think it's out of love that they don't spank are forming their decisions from worldliness and selfishness and not the Bible. Believe me, we feel the despair in needing to do it as well, but I didn't make myself or my children, therefore I must trust to the Creator's knowledge of His own designs, and not my feelings. When God says that we hate our children when we spare the rod, then that must be what we are doing. "He who spares his rod hates his son, but he that loves him, chastens him betimes" (often, promptly) (Proverbs 13:24). Not administering due consequences is like telling your child you give up on him/her, and he/she is not worth the time and effort of teaching. "Foolishness is bound in the heart of a child, but the rod of correction shall drive it far from him" (Proverbs 22:15). Again our instruction manual tells us what to expect, the solution to the problem, and the instrument for long term results.

"Yah, but they are too young to understand" you say? That's exactly why you biblically train early. You'll find with a solid biblical foundation, the blocks of education, work, business, life, etc. will stand stronger, and not fall away so easily. Why else are these early years so important? Proverbs 19:18 explains the need to "chasten thy son while there is hope, and let not thy soul spare for his crying." A young man or woman is already set in his/her ways and too old to begin. The greatest hope lies in the early years. From one earthly parent to another, let's admit it. Those pitiful tears wreak havoc on our heart strings. Several times I have had to chant to myself, "God's way is best. God's way is best. He alone knows the most successful development plan for my child." We have necessarily explained to them that it's hard as parents to have to spank them, but we too must obey the scriptures. Then, we trust the rest to God for the increase. Proverbs 23:12 extends reasoning help toward the weak willed parent: "Apply your heart to instruction and ears to words of knowledge; do not withhold correction from your child, for if thou beat him with a rod, he shall not die. Thou shall beat him with a rod, and deliver his soul from hell." Wow! How sympathetic our Father in Heaven is, to even supply us with "why" it's the rod. God will use controlled parents, with this simple rod as a vessel, to save our children from hell! Why argue further? As parents, we should be our children's greatest supporters and encouragers toward an eternal life and a physical life full of happiness, love, health, and blessings. It's true there are those who abuse their children, but don't let what someone else did wrong stop you from your own responsibility of obedience. God will take care of all vengeance that's necessary, as well as reward you for following Him amidst the persecutions of the world. Also, if you died to self for Christ to live in you instead, then there's no self to be offended if someone stereotypes you as an abuser. Too, if you died to self for Christ to live in you instead, then there's no self to get angry or impulsive. Don't even shrink because the Word says "beat," for you know that God did not imply that to mean abuse. Praise God and obey onward. It's you God wants to use to bring your children to a saving knowledge of grace through Jesus Christ, and He's telling you how to do it.

Keeping your children in your shadow not only allows you to shield their tender souls under good influence, but keeps you available to correct, and to guide their words and behavior before they become a problem. Use the rod to break a rebellious heart and attitude, to teach, or cleanse a child from willfulness and disobedience and a guilty conscience. Use of the rod has not only given rest and satisfaction to us as in Proverbs 29:17, but to the children as well.

Some basic guidelines we aim for are to correct at the first offense, deliver consequences without disappointed or angry feelings, instruct in scripture, and encourage. Any apologies necessary need to be delivered. Praying with the child is pertinent at times, and forgiveness of all parties must be seen through. This includes parents toward the children as well, even if the offense wasn't at them. Sometimes a child's disturbance, inconvenient interruption, lack of understanding, or lack of learning can plant seeds of bitterness in us. Not all the time, but sometimes the temptation arises. Realizing that we act to God as our children act to us should help us forgive them. When we who don't always have the right heart or attitude, or when we sin, procrastinate, are not punctual, complain, or interrupt others, remember how our God has patiently borne with us. Administer discipline promptly before behavior patterns develop. Clearly explain their offense without emotional severity. If you don't correct until the third or fourth time when your tone is now exalted, then you will inevitably train your child to understand you don't expect obedience until the third or fourth time or until your voice reaches that pitch and your face is all contorted.

Last, Psalm 51:7-12 sets a precedent to us that you should remain with your child until your relationship is restored. When parents use high emotions, irritations, and anger, or send the child to another room after wrong has been done, it tells the child, "I don't like you!" Rather, the message that needs to be sent is your intolerance of the sin committed. When a controlled parent dutifully and firmly sets the reproof, it's still understood they are loved, but the thing they *did* was wrong.

Children also learn what honesty is through our training. We are their first example of not lying. If we say something and don't immediately follow up or see it through, they learn words have no effect. "Yes" doesn't mean "yes," and "no" really doesn't mean "no." It's a very dangerous stumbling block for their young feet. Believe me, God's words are powerfully real and true, and thus ours should be, too.

A big difference with our family is we are a team, helping each other to the finish line of faith. The children understand this. When God blesses us with a new baby, it's another team member for all of us, which adds to our strength. We believe that if fathers obey God's written word, and mothers obey their husbands, and the whole family reads and lives the Bible together, then the children would follow with understanding. It's not enough to try and teach them religion and to go to church once a week. It's everything to show them by word, act, and deed, the love and excitement of God and His Bible every hour of every day. As for child training, do you want to gamble with their souls, trying to find some metaphor to the scriptures merely to rationalize an exemption from using the rod? Perhaps the alternate route is due to a sin of your own. Maybe not controlling your emotions? Perhaps it's due to persecution or from a vain desire to feel needed, loved, or loving in the world's eyes? Bribery will get results too, but it still is self-centered. Can God use other routes (like for fostering or adopting children)? Yes, it just won't be as easy.

Read 1 Corinthians chapter 13: if anything is done without love, it is nothing. We have to die to self and live as a temple for Christ's love to flow in, and then out. Therefore, the recipe for child training is God's love in you first, God's love through you second.

Please don't think it's all about your children, either, or you'll make them self-centered. With them, you always seek God first (this is how you can have a single income and make it just fine), and *with them* you compassionately and passionately seek to allow God to love others through you, by finding and serving their needs, opening your doors and being hospitable, sharing your bread, praying with them, and saying encouraging words to people around you. Be happy and rejoice while letting Christ love through you, and your children will be attracted to your life in Christ. And remember, play with your children

Although our children are not grown up yet, the vision we hold under God has provided good fruit so far. In the meantime, your prayers for us and ours would be counted as a blessing.

CHAPTER 22

Exorcisms and our Free Will

This account shares some very detailed descriptions during an exorcism and of spiritual manifestations. Please take caution concerning children and their maturity level for understanding. Also, the identity and certain aspects of the character involved has been changed for privacy and protection, however the circumstances remain true.

Remember chapter 12, *Victory over Darkness*? Let's take that knowledge and add another layer. How about personally witnessing demonic manifestations as they speak lies and threats? No, don't panic. I don't want you to focus and exalt the wicked side, but rejoice instead in the power and victory offered to all of us! Just realize that no devil can do anything when we have faith in Jesus.

Today, we clearly understand the feelings when the "seventy returned with joy, saying, Lord, even the devils are subject unto us through thy name" (Luke 10: 17-20). And we equally regard our Lord's answer to them when he said, "I beheld Satan as lightning fall from heaven. Behold, I give unto you power to tread on serpents and scorpions, and over all the power of the enemy: and nothing shall by any means hurt you. Notwithstanding in this rejoice not, that the spirits are subject unto you; but rather rejoice, because your names are written in heaven." This gentle counsel prevents self-righteousness.

This period in our lives began upon returning home from a three week mission of caretaking for family. As we rejoiced over miracles and blessings (such as how God again deposited $170 in our account), we implored God to continue to use us. Isaiah 58:4-12 seemed to be a recurrent word which told us "...to loose the bands of wickedness, to undo the heavy burdens, and to let the oppressed go free, and that ye break every yoke...deal thy bread to the hungry, and that thou bring the poor that are cast out to thy house...when thou seest the naked, that thou cover him; and that thou hide not thyself from thine own flesh..." We figured if God said do it, then He knows the varying associations, backgrounds, and characters that would be under our roof and with our children. Well, He brought to His house a most wonderful person.

Our new family member loved to sing, taught us wonderful new songs, cooked well, and we shared great times playing Scrabble and Yahtzee together with the children. She even helped introduce the youngest to the alphabet. However, she was often tormented by unclean spirits. What had once begun as thoughts became deceptions which grew until she audibly heard voices say profane murderous things, including ours. I'm so grateful the book of Ephesians (6:10-17) warns us, "For we wrestle not against flesh and blood, but against principalities, against powers, against the rulers of the darkness of this world, against spiritual wickedness in high places."

Another awesome thing about spiritual warfare...it's not hands-on combat. When people brought to Jesus 'many that were possessed with devils, He cast out the spirits with *His word* (emphasis mine), and healed all that were sick' (Mathew 8:16). This is our example to pursue. Following Jesus' death on the cross, the Authority and Anointing that was all passed down to Him, He in turn gave to us to carry on. We only need to believe. Also, we know God exalted His Son and gave Him a name "above every name: That at the *name of Jesus* (emphasis mine) every knee should bow, of things in heaven, and things in earth, and things under the earth" (Philippians 2:10). When we are working from a position of authority and faith, the Word tells us *nothing* is impossible. Did you notice that? It is IMPOSSIBLE for NOTHING to happen! (Isaiah 53; Matthew 7:7, 17:20, 21:21; Mark 11:23-26, 16:14-18; Luke 17:6, 11:9-10; John 14:12-14, 15:7, 16:24; James 1:5-9)

About the third day of her stay, after the children were in bed, this sweet lady was attacked again. I walked into the kitchen where Luke was patiently listening to her vent wicked accusations, which had grown from the last stories. I, only steps inside, in Jesus' name, rebuked Satan and his lying deceptive evil spirits and commanded them out of Sarah. Everything quieted down, and Luke and I left for bed. On the way, God was telling us to not leave her, to "get back down there quickly." Luke returned to find terror had possessed our guest. Thankfully, God was very present. Once more, I entered and as Luke offered that she was scared, I saw her squatted on the floor in the fetal position. The Holy Spirit moved me to again order Satan out of Sarah, "Right now! She is bought with a price and she's not yours!" God was fighting for His daughter! I felt such jealousy over anything having Sarah but God's love! Well, upon my command, Sarah leapt up screaming with her eyes rolled back in her head. The propulsion had her stumbling backwards until she contacted the wall. Luke hurried over in time to support her while she lay down on the floor.

Then, for the next three hours, we continued praying, singing, and reading the Bible, right there next to her. We sang about Jesus' blessed name, His wonderful blood, and praises of all kinds. God would lead us from one spot in the Bible to another. We found the last chapters of the gospels, especially Mark, were particularly offensive to the demons: "Go ye into all the world, and preach the gospel to every creature (I love how this says creature!). He that believeth and is baptized shall be saved; but he that believeth not shall be damned. And these signs shall follow them that believe; In my name shall they cast out devils; they shall speak with new tongues; They shall take up serpents; and if they drink any deadly thing, it shall not hurt them; they shall lay hands on the sick, and they shall recover" (Mark 16:15-20). A few times, upon reading these verses, the devils would lunge from the lying down position to attempt choking Luke, with hateful proclamations, things Sarah would never say. Luke, loving Sarah, and knowing where his power comes from, took no offense. Each time he'd hold her hands while claiming her back as God's daughter in Jesus' name. Quickly, the attack would subside and Sarah would lie back down, eyes closed and calm.

An interesting thing to note here is how the demons wouldn't voluntarily look at Luke. More often than not, they would cover the eyes with a hand, or, face him with eyes clamped shut. Nevertheless, the blood and authority would win over and they would have to look at Luke, to listen. On several occasions, when her eyes would open, they were clouded completely over, gray and white—like a blind man's—and Satan would verbally make threats toward Sarah's life, in the third person, saying, "You can *never* have her, she's *mine!*" "She'll get in her truck and go wherever I'll tell her to!" "She'll *never* go to church or prophesy again," and the like. Each time an unclean spirit spoke, we merely had to command "silence, in Jesus' name!" Then, all coaxing, arguing, accusations, and intimidations would end.

In another instance, she suddenly rolled over and tightly gripped the table leg as though bars in a jail, and roared at me (my station was under the table, to give Sarah space to be comfortable and Luke room as well). After the opaque-eyed demon roared, it yelled in rage that we couldn't have her. I leaned forward at it and yelled back that she wasn't his, so get out. Luke silenced the spirit and read the Word, which is our real sword.

As we lifted "holy hands" to evict one spirit after another, Satan tried several deceptive tactics. One was to distract us with the cares of this world. It would tell us that our children needed us in a whiny, worried voice, but we answered it by the information that "our children are not alone. They are covered and sealed by Jesus' blood."

The next tactic was to instill fear. With a sinister expression, one locked its gaze upon me and I could sense something not right behind those eyes, resembling things crawling around. I watched it and God whispered matter-of-factly, "They're trying to use fear on you." A moment later, "Don't be fearful." But as I looked away, I found I couldn't look at it again and thought how it was so creepy. My Father said, "Rebuke the fear! Be bold enough to confess it and stand!" So, I came against it and quoted a few verses about whom we only fear. This trick was never used again.

Third, we were praying when it turned toward me and sneered triumphantly, "yooou dooon't eeeven know how to pray for your *own* kids!" We silenced it and thanked God that it's His Words and Jesus Christ that does the work. Intriguingly, this piece of information had recently been a thought of mine, of which I shared with no one. Thus, Satan just proved to me it was his condemning voice trying to weaken my faith. This was a very exciting bit of evidence!

Finally, there was an incident where the temptation for vanity could have been a problem. You see, I have an intermittent habit of transposing words in a sentence. Our family has a lot of fun with it. Well, upon the current situation, I made a mistake. I commanded *Jesus* out of her. The cloudy-eyed demon laughed hideously, and with a slight turn of its head, sneeringly confided to an unseen spirit next to him, "She said for Jesus to get out" and chuckled again. Upon realizing what I spoke, I too broke into short laughter and praised God that Jesus' living blood isn't dependent upon my perfectly stated words. Satan then tersely snapped its mocking mouth shut and violently turned to face the wall as though a rebellious child.

Shortly afterward, one more wriggling display ensued before she slumped and looked relaxed. When peace was at hand, we called a pastor for some advice and felt confirmed the storm had passed. The entire time, our children slept soundly and never heard any of it! In the living room, afterward, Sarah only remembered three things. One, she described how she saw and felt the demon jump into her when we first left. Secondly, she shared it was as though she was in a submarine because she couldn't look through her own eyes, and, she remembers telling Luke to anoint her at the end. That night she, with us, praised Jesus for the victory and the freedom she had.

I don't believe casting out demons has to be an ordeal like this. It sure wasn't for Jesus and that's how we ought to walk (1John 2:6). We definitely need to press on toward more faith! I know God will help us grow so the next time, we, through our sweet Lord, can be more effective.

We tried to fill Sarah's new void with God's love for her and the Word, but Sarah had been living her deceived reality for over fifteen solitary years. It wasn't terribly long that we noticed the enemy come in at night and coax her back to him. Every attack after this, Luke handled. He simply had to rebuke Satan's lies and order him out. Twice, these circumstances lasted around fifteen minutes. These were the moments it would again straighten up to manifest itself, like a puffed up lizard. Using Sarah, the unclean spirits would make a powerful show lunging in an aggressive attack to strangle Luke. Mostly it was show, similar to a lion chained. It always seemed to lose its strength just before touching Luke. This is what made it so effortless for Luke to keep her hands captive. These attacks never came at me, and I believe God forbade them to do it, only allowing the demonstrations to go so far with Luke.

Through Matthew, we read a warning, "when the unclean spirit is gone out of a man, he walketh through dry places, seeking rest, and findeth none. Then, he saith, I will return into my house from whence I came out; when he is come, he findeth it empty, swept, and garnished. Then, goeth he, and taketh with himself seven other spirits more wicked than himself, and they enter in and dwell there: and the last state of that man is worse than the first. Even so, shall it be also unto this wicked generation" (Matthew 12:43-45). Sarah was exorcised and normal several times due to the Holy Spirit both by us and another church family. But, sadly enough, she did not want to walk as a new creature. She literally stated as much. So, she would return to her past to drudge up one situation after another. Rehearsing it, regretting it, trying to apply reasoning to it; and soon be repeating the ever-twisting, ever-growing falsehoods, and evil accusations. No matter how much we stated or showed her in scripture how much she was loved and how Jesus had set her free from her past by His death, she wouldn't believe it. Thus she protected the landing strip made by those evil spirits. Sarah now chose to live under her altered reality—never wishing to heed the dangers of entertaining devils when thinking negatively about herself or others.

Sarah really is a beautiful person. It's not a scar toward her that Satan wants to attack her. He is trying to destroy all of us. Rather, it shows how valuable and important she is.

The children and I had experienced complete peace thus far. In fact, the children wonderfully exemplified God's unbiased and unconditional love toward our welcome guest. In return, Sarah held a special love and bond for them that was precious to see. Luke and I both felt extremely blessed to see God work through our children's devotion and sympathy.

Upon the initial move over here we learned Sarah had a rifle she kept in her truck for protection and comfort. She was informed of our desire for it to be placed in storage instead of the house. However, perhaps a week into her stay, I awoke with the thoughtful information that she now had her gun in her bedroom. I, knowing Luke, did not mention anything about the matter until four weeks later, as he had faith in Jesus to protect us. If I had inquired of him, I would have heartily agreed. Thus, I wasn't concerned through these times.

However, there came a point in the end where her condition became much worse. She was now steadily angry and accusing. She would pace back and forth, vehemently muttering wickedness. At this point, I began to see the circumstances as bigger than God's power and Word. I became increasingly concerned about having her in our house with us. In spite of this, I had determined in my heart that she was welcome as long as God kept her there. We would not send her away, because God would not kick us away. If the gun were gone, I would have been fine. Finally, I inquired directly to Sarah concerning the matter, and she honestly admitted she had snuck her gun into her room, along with the ammunition. So, later that night we together brought the subject to Luke. He made the decision that this was about something bigger than fear and weapons.

I should have known Jesus was big enough. He demonstrated as much when she once paced nervously, muttering threats to us as we sat homeschooling at the dinner table. She hastily resolved to '*show us* and take care of it *herself*!' and rapidly went to her bedroom. I quickly moved around the kitchen table to place myself between the children and her, praying for God to stop her *now* and deliver her. I just arrived to the other side when Sarah suddenly popped out from around the corner and ever so sweetly said, "Oh, I wanted to ask what was for dinner and if I could help in any way." So, we began dinner preparations together. Yet, I couldn't get rid of the uneasiness from that point on.

It happened a few weeks later, when she decided, in a vexed attitude, to leave. But, she returned that night, and we welcomed her. We also reviewed house rules, such as controlling our thoughts with Philippians 4:8 and our tongue with Ephesians 4:29, 1 Corinthians 14:28, Psalm 71: 7-8, Romans 14:19, and similar verses. And, due to a shifting change in the situation a few days prior, Luke added the rule to escort the rifle into our locked storage. Sarah would not comply with that final request. She chose to leave that weekend, also pledging against ever getting help or taking medication.

It wasn't long before she was turned in, and committed. In all my Bible readings, I have never come across such titles as she was diagnosed with. Perhaps I need to read more, but all I can find are those possessed or tormented by unclean spirits, demons, and devils. The chemical imbalances are simply a physical manifestation of Satan's work, and not proof that it's not supernatural. These evil spirits are thieves at work in the world killing, stealing, and destroying (John 10:10). I'm so grateful God gave us Jesus "that we might have life, and life more abundantly" (John 10:10).

Since this narrative, we have met a man whose faith was much bigger than ours. He prayed with us over Sarah with hundreds of miles between us. A few days later we were told, she was happy and no delusions were spoken. The doctor removed some of her medications and she was released two days later, instead of the planned goal of ninety. After speaking with this gentleman, we can't help but wonder if the entire above account could have been different. But, I praise God for helping Sarah no matter how it happened, and for loving to use us anyhow.

The times we began to feel worn out, our loving Teacher showed us it was only because we were listening to our flesh. Selfishness doesn't want to "deal with" other people, especially in difficult situations. It was also due to *our* using our own reasoning rather than the scriptures. No matter what arrives in life, there is never a time to divert from Truth. The reason these cycles exist is free will. Our Creator gave us each a free will to make choices. Each individual seems to have his vices. Whether it is passiveness, bitterness, pride, lust, vanity, alcohol, or drugs, our free choice allows us to be liberated in Christ to love and live, as well as be chained, where we walk the same circle, always tethered to those vices and the world in one instance or another. But the blood of God's only Son can dissolve those shackles; it's not when you become a worthy person. "While we were yet sinners, He sent His only begotten son" (John 3:16). His gift of love for you is *that* personal! It's *that* deep and intimate! God loves you even though He knows all you've done! So quit hiding! Our loving Father in Heaven won't force it on you. Just remember that He knows you already, and is waiting for you to believe Him at His Word that *you* are so passionately loved that He sent 'His only begotten Son to die in your stead' (John 3:16). Your potential is only limited by yourself. Knowing who we are in God makes us so free! And to think we only know in part! (1 Corinthians 13:8-13) Wait until we grow!

I also glory in the fact that Luke had no income jobs the whole time Sarah was with us—except three hours per week cleaning the Post Office. God's work first, and He is always good about providing wages!

CHAPTER 23

Not the Beginning or the End,
Just the Middle

Hebrews 12:1-2 reads "[1]wherefore seeing we also are compassed about with so great a cloud of witnesses, let us lay aside every weight, and the sin which doth so easily beset us, and let us run with patience, the race that is set before us, [2]looking unto Jesus the author and finisher of our faith; who for the joy that was set before Him endured the cross, despising the shame, and is set down at the right hand of the throne of God." We definitely have a great number of witnesses from whom to learn and gain faith to help us run a race with patience. We are learning that the lack of patience—which means cheerful endurance—is due to a lack of love. Patience also implies diligence and perseverance for the longevity. This race is not a sprint, it is a marathon.

God, too, has a multigenerational vision. The "race" does not end with us. It must continue with our children. They, then, must train their children to run the race. In light of this "relay race" we want to send a baton with each child to symbolize in his or her family the continuation of a higher goal, to carry on the race with patience. This baton includes this book. This passing of the faith does not mean "we are done." Luke and I have very important roles as grandparents besides the follow-through of our own individual lives. However, a godly inheritance is the first to be passed on, and we pray this "baton" will always remind you of your part in the continuation of the race until our Lord and Savior returns on a cloud to call us all *home*.

In the past, God had done so much for the Israelites when He freed them from being captives, but nobody remembered. So, when he split the Jordan for them to cross over into their promised land, He commanded them to bring out twelve stones from the bottom of the Jordan River, "where the priests' feet stood firm" in the center. They carried those stones to their lodging places. "That this may be a sign among you, that when your children ask their fathers in time to come, saying, What mean ye by these stones? Then ye shall answer them, That the waters of Jordan were cut off before the ark of the covenant of the Lord; when it passed over Jordan, the waters of Jordan were cut off: and these stones shall be for a memorial unto the children of Israel for ever. And the children of Israel did so as Joshua commanded, and took up twelve stones out of the midst of Jordan, as the Lord spake unto Joshua, according to the number of the tribes of the children of Israel, and carried them over with them unto the place where they lodged, and laid them down there. And Joshua set up twelve stones in the midst of Jordan, in the place where the feet of the priests which bare the Ark of the Covenant stood: and they are there unto this day" (Joshua 4:6-9). This book is intended as a memorial stone, to track and remember the merciful blessings of our Heavenly Father. We have not written every miracle into these pages, but we pray the ones that were recorded will be a blessing for generations to come.

Finally, we both want to encourage *you* to remember: Remember to read your Bible, there may come a day when you are only allowed to have it in your mind. It is also the only way to know if what you see and hear in the world is Truth or not. Remember the *depth* of love in what Jesus Christ did for you and the free gift of salvation God offers you. Remember Jesus' death and the Anointing He passed on to His believers is not a selfish ticket to heaven, but the way to have the Kingdom of Heaven within us here on earth, to "love out" today. Remember to serve God and obey the commandments. Remember the beauty God created. Remember to hate the sin and not the sinner. Remember to stand for God, even in the little things. Those little things will shape your habit to stand when the big test comes. Remember to search diligently the scriptures to be fully persuaded in your own mind and be steadfast, but to not dispute. Remember to have a humble, open mind, ready to consider all things in prayer, as you will *always* be learning, never being "arrived" to know how God thinks. Remember, God is in control, there is no need to be fearful. Remember to have faith. Remember to have hope. Remember to love and love as God loves, not as the world loves. Remember to tithe. Remember to sing and rejoice. Remember to be joyful. Remember to be thankful! Remember that your life for God starts within the family, and then spreads out. You do not have a witness if you cannot love and honor your own family. Remember to disciple your children so they can teach their children. Remember that revivals are delayed when you don't remember the wondrous things God has done for you.

From here on, we will continue to learn until the Lord comes back. And perhaps, you will find a sequel sharing of many more children, and of God's blessed lessons and miracles. As an enticement, I must share a recent move of God: We met a gentleman using crutches. He also wore a knee cast, and was headed for surgery. We prayed with him. The next day he was free from the crutches. The second day, he was free from the knee brace! The third day we spoke with him, and he proclaimed no more pain! Jesus' death destroyed the work of the devil! He was healed!

Another case that I love was our town fire. The children and I prayed for the taverns/bars to shut down. One bar foreclosed and lost the liquor license. Two weeks later, we were awakened at 3:00 am. A second bar was engulfed in flames! Obviously, we *had* to wake the children to take them down to witness God's power!

If God wills there to be a continuation, we hope to also reveal His chosen future for our lives. Will it be our own house and land where our mission field will be town and community? Will he take us on a mission adventure somewhere else? Will we get to be mobile missionaries always forsaking a place to lay our heads for the glory of God? I know God has His plans in motion already. This we have left today at His feet, and He will unveil our future as we need to know. Pray for our family and God's guidance in our lives. We love you, and what is more important, God loves you.

"I will open my mouth in a parable: I will utter dark sayings of old: Which we have heard and known, and our fathers have told us. We will not hide them from their children, showing to the generations to come the praises of the Lord, and his strength, and his wonderful works that he hath done. For he established a testimony in Jacob, and appointed a law in Israel, which he commanded our father, that they should make them known to their children: That the generation to come might know them, even the children which should be born; who should arise and declare them to their children: That they might set their hope in God, and not forget the works of God, but keep his commandments: And might not be as their fathers, a stubborn and rebellious generation; a generation that set not their heart aright, and whose spirit was not steadfast with God…" ~ Psalm 78:2-8

"And thou shalt remember all the way which the Lord thy God led thee these forty years in the wilderness, to humble thee, and to prove thee, to know what was in thine heart, whether thou wouldest keep his commandments, or no" ~ Deuteronomy 8:2

"Give thanks unto the Lord, call upon His name, make known His deeds among the people. Sing unto Him, sing psalms unto Him, talk ye of all His wondrous works. Glory ye in His holy name: let the heart of them rejoice that seek the Lord. Seek the Lord and His strength, seek His face continually. Remember His marvelous works that He hath done, His wonders, and the judgments of His mouth" 1Chronicles 16:8-12

Interview with my dearly beloved Lucas Munsen

To our future generations

What helps a husband and wife be "one"? How about spiritually one?

- *Both spouses need to love God above anything else and draw all their needs from Him. In this way they can truly be one, without worldly pressures and expectations.*
- *Be considerate, love her as you love yourself*
- *Pray together*
- *Study together*
- *Talk/dream/plan together, keep the communication open even if it means being vulnerable*
- *Embrace her every day*

How do you see a wife can reverence her husband?

- *A wife reverences her husband by discussing her plans and thoughts with him. Even if he doesn't have answers, they can together search them out prayerfully. Not as to a chauvinist, but in respect and loving oneness*
- *Husbands like the respect of their wife coming to them first.*
- *Smile!*
- *Have faith in him and his ideas.*

What advice do you have for our future husbands?

- *A man has to find their wife's talents and abilities and put them to use to help her be fulfilled. Encourage her in the areas she is strongest and take up the slack where she is weak.*

- *Be one with her.*

What advice do you have for future fathers?

- *Remember to spend time with your children, to tie strings with them,*
- *Win their hearts by reading stories, bouncing them to bed, playing with them, etc.*
- *Discuss important things with them.*
- *Share plans/dreams/decisions with them. Open your heart to them.*
- *Love them and speak to them respectfully*
- *Discipline them as part of discipling them.*
- *Don't hide your short-comings from them, always be honest and let them see you overcome through your faith in God.*

What do you mean, "win their heart"?

- *It means they will love you and want to follow you and your ways as you follow and obey God's statutes and commandments.*
- *Winning their hearts will only come when they see that you love them in word and deed, and want to spend time with them.*
- *It means they want to be like you.*

What summary of advice do you have for training children?

- *Be diligent with switching, but never switch with anger or too much emotion*
- *Following each use of the rod they have to understand it is done out of love for them and based on the Bible so they know where your authority comes from.*
- *Pray with them.*

- *Know the above is ineffective unless you are tying strings of love.*

What's your summary on biblical patriarchy?
- *I don't believe fathers should be away from their family eight to ten hours a day, they need to be able to take their sons with them, to be available to the family for guidance, leadership, discipline, and encouragement. You can't make your family obey you, but you can lead them to Jesus, who is worthy of our obedience.*
- *Fathers should try to have a self-employed/family business. Something to pass on to their children.*
- *Don't chase money, chase God.*

What summary or advice do you have concerning debt?
- *To live with your parents until you can save enough to start with your own land/home and even if it's meager.*
- *Believe the Bible when it says to owe no man anything. Staying out of debt, not using credit, etc, is God's best for you*
- *Don't get involved with a woman until you are established. Until you have a nest/nest egg to offer her. Until you have paid the bride-price. Then she will be worth more to you as well.*

What is your opinion of education?
- *Read lots of books when young as responsibilities of adult life leave much less time to do this.*
- *Prove everything with the Bible.*
- *Education is from whole books, life books, life lessons, not meaningless facts.*
- *I encourage reading biographies of Godly men.*

What are your expectations of the children when they are ten to twelve years old?

- To put in a hard day's work and know how to take care of themselves
- To be about the business of adults
- Wanting and seeking wisdom from the Bible and their elders

What about tithe?

- Top priority is to tithe 10% before you think of anything else or you run the risk of not being a cheerful giver or running out of money to tithe with.
- In the end, you will tithe no matter what. You have the choice to cheerfully tithe to God, or God will allow the devourer to come and take it through abnormal costs like doctor bills, mechanic bills, loss, repairs, maintenance, etc. etc. and you'll miss out on His blessing. Really, you can't afford to not tithe.

If you had to sum up life in one exhortation, what would it be?

- Obey the written Holy Word, the Bible, and depend upon and follow God
- Marry a godly wife!

Is there anything else you want the next generations to know?

- Watch out for pride!
- Be humble in everything!
- Give thanks always!
- Do not hold ANY book up alongside the Bible.

Luke's On-the-Mountain Prayer Notes

During this phase in our life (see chapter 11), Luke decided to spend some one-on-one time with his Heavenly Father in his favorite spot—the mountains. He came home several days later with answers on Sabbath days, debt versus cash, and family responsibilities and assignments. His notes are recorded for your perusal.

New Testament/New Covenant

Matthew chapter 5, verse 17 and 18

"Think not that I am come to destroy the law, or the prophets: I am not come to destroy, but to <u>fulfill</u>. For verily I say unto you, till heaven and earth pass, one jot or one tittle shall in no wise pass from the law till all be fulfilled."

- Jesus fulfilled the sacrifice. He is our eternal sacrifice. We are no longer saved through continual sacrifice; the price has been paid, once, for all.
- We no longer need an earthly priest. Jesus is our eternal priest and mediator.
- Jesus fulfilled the Sabbath rest. He is our Sabbath rest.
- However, the Sabbath is not legalistic works, but rest. It is a privilege and gift from God to help us realign our priorities for the next week, as well as recuperate from the previous week. A special time to meet up with our God and spend a day with Him.

Debt

I.   Debtor is servant to the lender

    a.   A Christian is to be a servant of God, not debt. When serving debt nobody can be ultimately free to change course in life instantly when God needs them to perform special assignments.

b. <u>Matthew chapter 6 verse 24 through 25</u>: "No man can serve two masters: for either he will hate the one, and love the other; or else hold to the one and despise the other. Ye cannot serve God and money" (ie: debt).

c. Conclusion: Debt is not an option. It's not God's best for His children. We need to have contentment and faith in His timing and provisions.

II. Put faith in God, not money

a. <u>Matthew chapter 6 verse 31 through 33</u>: "Therefore take no thought, saying, what shall we eat? Or what shall we drink? Or wherewithal shall we be clothed? [For all these things do the Gentiles seek] for your heavenly Father knoweth that ye have need of all these things. But seek ye first the kingdom of God and His righteousness; and all these things shall be added unto you.

1. Jesus didn't say seek the kingdom first, and then seek food and clothing. He said "all these things shall be added unto you". Praise is to God! Live for God's work—spreading His love—and He will see we have no lack.

III. If you are already in debt God is merciful. Repent, and ask for deliverance. Purpose to *never* do it again. God's ways are not our ways (Isaiah 55:8).

IV. Other truths and laws about money and debt.

a. Charging interest to another Christian is prohibited

1. A loan should be an act of kindness. It should be

given with no expectation to receive it back. Only God has the control whether it comes back or not.

b. God wants me to keep His money among His children
   1. Patronize Christian businesses

Godly Stewardship over My Family

I. As Christ will never leave or forsake the church, I must never leave or forsake my wife or my family.

a. The only times Christ left his disciples was to be alone with God
   1. The disciples left and forsook Him when he was being accused and crucified, but Christ received them back.

b. I must be available to protect, provide, instruct, and "cleanse" my family.
   1. I cleanse because the sins of my family are translated to me as my sins are translated to Christ.

c. I must cleave to my wife, we are one flesh. I must realize I need her. I need to include her and nurture her.
   1. Christ never leaves his church, God never leaves His Son.
      i. John chapter 8 verse 29: "He that sent me is with me: the Father has not left me alone, for I do all those things that please Him."

d. I must disciple the boys and my wife must disciple the girls (this does not mean I am not involved in my girls' life, but it takes their mother to teach them womanly things).
   1. They must see all that we do as Jesus' disciples saw all that He did.

    2. We must teach our children God's Ways—and Words—and show them His Spirit through our walk, our example.

        i. We must teach our children to teach their children.

II. Conclusion: God does not want me to leave my family eight hours a day to work for a corporation. I must find ways to work from home, to be that daddy that God wants of me. By God's grace, mercy, and love, I see it is my God-given purpose to be self-employed—working where God directs me and having the freedom to be available for my family at any time.

Character Qualities

It's very important for parents to search ways to praise the good character qualities of their children. However, you will be your own enemy if you praise vain things, thus building up "pride" and "self". By these I mean, "you're so smart!", or "you're so pretty!" Below, you will find a list of character qualities. Find out what these mean and use them instead. Your children will benefit greatly when you praise their "attentiveness" when learning, and their "diligence" to finish their work. This doubles by adding to their vocabulary lessons as well. Search ways to praise the good ten times more than you need to correct them. This will save you from having so many corrections and allows you to lead them into good behavior habits with love and fun.

Alertness	Attentiveness	Availability
Benevolence	Boldness	Brotherly Kindness
Cautiousness	Charity	Commitment
Compassion	Contentment	Creativity
Decisiveness	Dependability	Determination
Diligence	Discernment	Discretion
Endurance	Enthusiasm	Faith
Flexibility	Forbearance	Forgiveness
Generosity	Gentleness	Godliness
Gratefulness	Holiness	Honor
Hospitality	Humility	Initiative
Joyfulness	Justice	Loyalty
Meekness	Obedience	Orderliness
Patience	Persuasiveness	Prudence
Punctuality	Reconciliation	Resourcefulness
Responsibility	Security	Sensitivity
Temperance	Thoroughness	Thriftiness
Tolerance	Truthfulness	Virtue
Wisdom		

A Few Fun Home Remedies
and Other Recipes

My Garlic Antibiotic Infused Oil Rub where it ails ya!
Macerate at least 4 oz fresh garlic (from the store is fine). Cover garlic/herbs with 1 pint olive oil or grape seed oil in a non-aluminum/cast iron pan. Gently heat the mixture, uncovered, for 1 hour on the lowest possible setting. Don't let it get hotter than 190 degrees F. Pour oil and herbs into a jar and seal tightly and steep for 2 weeks, shaking daily. Strain the oil, put into a clean jar, and store in a dark place. (The directions are the same for other infused oils. Just replace the fresh garlic for fresh herbs of your choice, or use 2 oz dried herbs instead).

My Garlic Antibiotic Salve I rub it on the feet and neck of my children when a sickness threatens.
Perform the above infused garlic oil. When ready add .4 ounce grated beeswax per ½ cup garlic infused oil (or any herbal infused oil) to sauce pot. Heat gently until beeswax is melted. Do not heat enough to bubble or you may lose properties in the oil. Stir and allow to slightly cool. Pour mixture into jar while still warm (I use a half-pint wide mouth). Close jars tightly and allow it to set.

My Homemade Toothpaste

14	tsp	aluminum-free baking soda
3	tsp	sea salt (not course ground) – optional
1/8	tsp	Peppermint Extract Flavor (optional or any other flavor desired)

1. Mix baking soda, salt, and flavoring
2. Place in container or old salt shaker and use

Note: This recipe may not taste the best until you get used to it, but it's great for healthy teeth.

My Homemade Lip Balm Makes approx. 2 ¼ ounces. Small ointment jars work great!

.4	oz	beeswax
1/4	c	grape seed oil/olive oil
1/4	tsp+	vitamin E oil
1/4	tsp+	essential oil/extract flavoring

Combine beeswax, grape seed oil, and vitamin E oil in a small, pourable container (a glass measuring cup works well). Place this container in a saucepan—on top of a canning ring—filled with water halfway up the glass cup. Simmer until beeswax is completely liquefied. Remove from heat and add essential oil. Pour into container. Cool completely before use.

Homemade Recipe for Laundry Soap

Ingredients:

- 1-2 bars of soap (a soap of any choice)
- 1 cup "20 Mule Team Borax"
- ½ cup Arm & Hammer Super washing Soda (or baking soda)
- Water

Tools:

- 5 Gallon container
- Knife/Pot/Saucepan
- Long stirring stick/spoon (for the 5 gallon container)

Instructions:

Pour 5 cups of water in the pot and heat it just shy of boiling. You want the water hot enough to be able to melt the soap, but not hot enough to boil over. While the water is warming up, use the knife (or cheese grater) to cut the bar of soap into small strips. Add the shredded soap to the pot of heated water. Stir the mixture until the soap is completely melted.

Once the soap is melted, pour 3 gallons of **hot water** into the 5 gallon container. To the 3 gallons of hot water you'll stir in the melted soap mixture. Once it's adequately mixed, add the ½ cup of washing soda (or baking soda) and stir until dissolved. Once the washing soda is completely dissolved, pour in the cup of Borax and stir again until completely dissolved.

Now that everything is mixed and dissolved, you'll have a 5-gallon container of soapy water. Cover the container, and place it somewhere it won't be disturbed. Let it cool overnight. It will begin to gel as it cools. However it will not gel uniformly so if you see lumpy watery gel, don't be alarmed. You may store your soap in smaller containers.

Optional:
- If you prefer, you may add a few drops of essential oils for a pleasant scent.

Amount per Load:

½-1 cup is sufficient to clean a normal load of clothes, but may use 1-2 cup for heavily soiled or a fuller load. This recipe is great for high efficiency washing machines because it is a low sudsing detergent. (A word of warning for High Efficiency Machines: before pouring the lumpy gel into the detergent dispenser, stir with a spoon, pencil, finger, or whatever to break up the lumps. Very large lumps may not fully dissolve)

Laundry Softener:
- I add white distilled vinegar to softener dispenser to remove soap residue, for an antibacterial rinse, and for sensitive skin (great for baby cloth diapers)

Dearest Friends,

You have listened to our testimonies, now we are excited to hear yours. Please mail us your story, review, accounts, or comments at the email address below. All feedback is greatly appreciated and welcome.

Please don't send me any solicitations, crude contents, services, or advertisements; I would consider this a violating use of my address. I thank you for your honesty and understanding in this matter.

Looking forward to hearing from you,
Roxanne and Luke Munsen, and six little disciples (so far)

EMAIL ADDRESS:
rememberfeedback@outlook.com

Want to know about family or ministry updates? Then please visit westbowpress.com to find my personal website, either by book title or author. Here you may find occasional updates, blogs, as well as other information.

22620888R00141

Printed in Great Britain
by Amazon